READYMADE
BUSINESS LETTERS
THAT GET RESULTS

The Daily Express Guides

The Daily Express and Kogan Page have joined forces to publish a series of practical guides offering no-nonsense advice on a wide range of financial, legal and business topics.

Whether you want to manage your money better, make more money, get a new business idea off the ground – and make sure its legal – there's a Daily Express Guide for you.

Titles published so far are:

Great Ideas for Making Money
Niki Chesworth

Your Money
How to Make the Most of it
Niki Chesworth

You and the Law
A Simple Guide to All Your Legal Problems
Susan Singleton

How to Cut Your Tax Bill Without Breaking the Law
Grant Thornton, Chartered Accountants

Be Your Own Boss!
How to Set Up a Successful Small Business
David Mc Mullan

Readymade Business Letters That Get Results
Jim Douglas

Available from all good bookshops, or to obtain further information please contact the publishers at the address below:

Kogan Page Ltd
120 Pentonville Rd
London N1 9JN
Tel: 071-278 0433
Fax: 071-837 6348

Daily Express

READYMADE BUSINESS LETTERS THAT GET RESULTS

Second Edition

JIM DOUGLAS

KOGAN PAGE

Author's Note

Readers are encouraged to write personal letters based on the examples in this book. This in no way permits the infringement of copyright, and the prior written permission of the publisher is necessary for the reproduction of multiple copies.

First published in 1986 entitled *Readymade Business Letters*
© Avebury Publishing Co Ltd 1986
Second edition 1994 by Jim Douglas
© Jim Douglas 1994

Kogan Page Limited
120 Pentonville Road
London N1 9JN

British Library Cataloguing in Publication Data

A CIP record for this book is available from the British Library.

ISBN 0-7494-1186-4 (P/bk)

ISBN 0-7494-1365-4 (H/bk)

Typeset by Books Unlimited (Nottm), Sutton-in-Ashfield, NG17 1AL

Printed and bound in Great Britain by Clays Ltd, St Ives plc

Contents

Part 1:

Introduction

There are two rules with business letters:

- minimise them;
- utilise them.

In other words, keep them as few and as short as you can – but take advantage of them. The business letter helps you to organise situations the way you want. You can keep your company profitable, increase sales, set up new ventures, enjoy good working friendships, all through your business letters.

How often people complain about their correspondence. How overwhelmed they are with the burden of composing complex narratives or underwhelmed with churning out repetitive trivia. How every morning a pile of envelopes waits on their desks, and every afternoon a renewed mountain of filing remains to be hidden away.

Examine your correspondence, and why you write to people, and they to you. If you look through old correspondence, and indeed old textbooks of business correspondence, you find letters appear wordy and elaborate – such was the style of those days. There seems to be a tradition dating from when business letters were crafted in copperplate by aged myopic gentlemen straight out of Dickens sitting at high desks. 'We beg to acknowledge receipt of your esteemed order,' they begin, and eventually conclude, 'Assuring you of our best attention at all times, and oblige.' The ending being an obscure grammatical usage which sounds vaguely suggestive.

True, it's difficult to be brilliantly witty when you have to write Dear mr brown our april account £479.83 is still unpaid if you don't settle within seven days we shall have no choice but to cancel your credit status and demand pre-payment for further supply – for the umpteenth month on the trot. But you know what we mean. You have your firm's performance and reputation to uphold by the quality of your letters. And even if you don't care about that, you have your self-respect.

If you finish the day thinking, I've written some good letters with some good twists in them (perhaps the one with the poem will get that £479 out of old Brown) – that's better than drifting home depressed by another day of drivel and drudgery. Let a bit of spirit enter into your letters.

Don't neglect the timing of your letters. Particular letters entail their own seasons – sales letters may be geared to setting up the pre-Christmas market; credit control letters go out according to a regular system. Other exchanges of letters may depend on other sets of rules. For courtesy, you reply by return. But to pick up a favourable contract you may want to delay writing – if only so that it looks as if you have pondered your proposal. Then there are complex situations where a hasty reply would be ill-considered; the best course of action will mature in your mind with a week or two of delay.

If you are the employer, you are responsible for the letters written by your staff – that is, you are liable for the consequences. So if an employee sends out a quotation with a nought missed off, you may have to live with it, although usually you can apologise and start again.

The business letter can achieve a great deal. Out of the blue you can write to strangers and strike up acquaintances, set up deals, correspond for years. You can have pen pals, not to say epistolary romances.

Letters, time and overhead costs

A letter can do the trick – all for the cost of a postage stamp, they say.

Business letters cost more than a postage stamp. You can work it out. If you are in that curious, pampered position of having a secretary to type your letters, add up the cost of your salary plus hers for the five or ten minutes of dictation, or the time for you to scribble it out, plus 10 or 15 minutes of her time for typing (or yours if you do it), plus the filing and looking for things, plus a slice of overhead cost for 20 minutes of office occupancy. Your letter has cost several pounds before you so much as stick a second-class stamp on it.

Letters become wondrously cheaper when secretaries are shared or hapless men have to type their own. Letters also become shorter and to the point, not to say fewer in the first place.

If you create your own letters on a word processor, you will be just as aware of the impact of time and cost. It costs less, in theory, for you to compose and print out your own letters than to have the luxury of a secretary or typist. But hours can pass, as in a dream, while you remember how to move paragraphs around without deleting your text, having of course accidentally deleted your text in the process. It is also better than work – it is a kind of pseudo-work – sitting there attending to your computer housekeeping, proudly gazing at your directory structure and changing a file name here and there.

Ask yourself, do you have to write at all? Don't acknowledge absolutely everything when there is no need. It's like trying to have the last word in a quest for good manners brownie points. There are alternatives to writing. You can telephone. Short calls do not necessarily cost more, and you can make instant contact.

You can also scribble, or shall we say neatly inscribe, upon your correspondent's letter and post or fax it straight back to him. Some people favour quaint stickers in Hollywoodesque script saying, 'Excuse the informality!! replying on your letter to get back to you sooner' – or words to that effect. If you like that sort of thing by all means write on the margins of letters and put them straight back in an envelope. It depends what they are, of course. On some letters you can write 'AGREED, Jim' – or 'OVER MY DEAD BODY J.D.' Do it, and see how it goes. If people stop writing to you, you will know you are cutting down your workload nicely. Or else you may cravenly decide your image is suffering, and start writing letters again on triple smoked salmon cartridge rag bond reading, 'Dear Maurice AGREED Kind regards Yours sincerely Jim', which will cost you £20 in overheads.

The other thing you can do is handwrite your reply on a compliments slip and staple that to the letter, putting both into the envelope. This course has a shade more cachet. You can always keep a photocopy of your terse rejoinder.

Setting the tone

When you have decided to write to someone or reply to a letter, as distinct from ignoring it or composing graffiti on it, you come to the question of the appearance of the letter, its image and its tone.

The business letter conveys vital messages to its recipient in all sorts of ways: the paper it is written on, the design of the letterhead (see illustration), the layout of the typing. These elements may be beyond your control and you may have to work within the confines of corporate style, but be aware of the visual impact of your communications.

And as for how you actually write it – the crisp yet flowing style; punchy brevity combined with lyrical powers of description when

'THE WEAVERHAM'

DRILLING, MILLING, FILING,
ROLLING, PRESSING, GRINDING,
MACHINING & SUNDRIES CO.
LTD

All
types of
machinery
undertaken
Steel
stockist
Drop
forging
Welding
Second
hand
railway
wagons
Nuts
bolts
washers

"We work for our pleasure
and your profit"

Trafalgar Works
Sebastopol St.
Ormskirk, Lancs.

MEDAL
LEIPZIG
1847

HONOUR
PARIS
1888

PRIZE
REYKJAVIK
1901

Founded 1817
Directors XXXXXXXXXX

"We solder on regardless"

An old-fashioned letterhead. Not much
room to write but a good read.

THE
RASTIGNAC-de LESSEPS BUILDING
LONDON, W.

A posh letterhead. No one knows who it's
from.

 TITAN

Corporate HQ   Northsea House
King William Street   London EC3 4QQ

A modern letterhead suffering from corporate image and incomprehensible logo.

IMPECCABLE RESOURCES
CORPORATION
1 WATLING ST. LAYBY
MILTON FEIGNS
BUCKS
Tel. XXXXX Fax. XXXXX

Directors XXXXXXXXXXXX
Regd. office XXXXXXXXXXXX
Chief letter writer P. Erson

A letterhead like you probably have. OK
until a director gets fired. Then you have to
type XXXXX over his name every time.

Different models of letterhead design

some little detail needs elaborating; strong persuasive prose, illumined by shafts of sardonic observation and mordant, yet compassionate, wit. Yes. All that will come.

Layout and planning of your letter

The commonest layout for the business letter today is known as the blocked style. In this style all new lines of typing are ranged to the left and punctuation is dispensed with in the address and the greetings. This streamlining is designed to save the typist time. The same style is followed on the envelope.

The most frequently seen alternative arrangement is the indented style which indents new paragraphs and punctuates the address and greetings. This layout now has a traditional appearance as against the thrusting, modern, slightly brutalist effect of the blocked style. Your private correspondence looks better indented.

By all means lay out your letters to look different if you wish, such as by putting your sign-off on the right instead of the left or putting the destinatee at the bottom instead of the top. But remember, fancy variations are obstacles to instant communication. We would dearly like you to turn your business life into an art form, but if you want your letters to be read and indeed answered you have to speak the recipient's language. Otherwise you increase the risk of your letters being:

(a) crumpled up derisively and cast into the wpb;
(b) chuckled over knowingly with the remark, 'Old Jim's at it again';
(c) framed and auctioned for charity.

The latter eventuality may be remote in your case, even though you have read that Salvador Dali once discovered he could sell his autograph on a blank sheet of paper for a lot of money and began whipping off thousands of signatures, like you and I sign piles of direct mail letters to make them look individualised.

You may have a brilliantly retentive grasp of details, like Mozart who was able to write down a balance sheet* he heard played once in St Peter's, Rome; or like the tycoons interviewed in the Sunday paper who have just added £400m to their personal fortune in an

---

* This should read: canon

arbitrage coup while we were writing business letters. If you can't remember everything you are meant to say in the right order, you plan your letter by noting down the points to be covered, whether by assembling information on your desk or by picking them out of the correspondence you're replying to. If you are dictating your letter or if you are writing it out, some scribbled notes will be enough to provide a structure.

If you have to write the same sort of letter regularly, you will have a more or less standard structure to resort to. Credit letters follow a well-established pattern of escalating pressure on the late payer. Sales letters, in particular direct mail shots, have another classic structure, viz:

1. catch attention;
2. raise awareness of customer's need;
3. describe product to match the need;
4. clinch ordering action.

The basic rules and good practice

The basic rules entail starting and finishing letters in the usual, recognisable way. There is a tendency towards increasing informality of expression. First names are more freely used and old starchy formulae abandoned.

When you don't know the name of the person you're writing to, often when it is to an impersonal head of department, a government official or a bank officer, you begin: Dear Sir, and finish with: Yours faithfully. When you have the name of the person you are writing to and the letter is on a personal level, you write: Dear Mr...(or Mrs, or Miss, or Ms). When you begin with Dear Mr...or Dear Ms...etc, you finish with: Yours sincerely. If you don't know the person's name but you want to write a personal letter, you ring up his firm and ask his name (and initials). As far as you are able or aware, never get a name wrong. People get annoyed when they are misspelt. It's a good way to lose the order before they've read the letter.

If you are writing to a woman, especially in the USA, you can write Ms (pronounced miz), but in the UK it is still politer except in feminist circles to find out whether she is Mrs or Miss.

If you feel kindly disposed towards your recipient, you can add at the end of your letter, and before the yours sincerely, the formula 'best wishes' or 'kind regards'. There are many variants on this prac-

---

BUSINESS LETTERS – THE BASIC RULES ...

- Remember to date and sign your letters.
- Include the other party's reference if any.
- If you begin with 'Dear Sir' or 'Dear Madam', you end with 'Yours faithfully'.
- If you begin with 'Dear Mr...' or 'Dear Mrs...' or 'Dear Felicity', you end with 'Yours sincerely'.
- If replying to an earlier letter start with 'Thank you for your letter of ...'

... AND GOOD PRACTICE

- Plan your letter and set it out logically.
- Spell the recipient's name and address right – people hate their names being misspelt.
- Keep letters short – comfortably on one page.
- Put surplus matter in attachments to a covering letter, eg reports, proposals, contracts, lists.
- Maintain good relations by courteous language and expressing good wishes.
- Read through before sending and reject scruffy typing.
- Remember the enclosures if any.

---

tice, with varying nuances of meaning. In certain spheres of management it is virtually obligatory to end your letter with kind regards even though you detest the person.

Always quote the reference on your correspondent's letter if it has a useful purpose. References are vital if they serve:

(a) to track down the right individual in a large organisation;
(b) to identify a specific product or proposal;
(c) to keep the correspondence filed in the right place, especially for your correspondent, who is an extremely busy, important, sophisticated person and can't always remember where he put your last letter. Alternatively, or in addition, he may be your accountant or your lawyer and you may as well act in your own self-interest.

Such people tend to use reference systems such as 95-Per-0018/Q-Sp/PMT/06. You can readily invent your own. If you have just received your first export order for a million pairs of size 12 socks, you may like to lend the correspondence the dignity of a reference, and instruct your customer to quote Biggie/001.

You can ignore some references. If you get a letter from Michael Jones and the reference at the top reads MJ/kb, all this tells you is that his secretary is called Katie Brown or Krystal Borl. Sometimes firms have typing pools so kb would identify the hapless creature responsible for mishearing what he said on his audio.

References usually go at the top right just above the date. You can sometimes quote a reference in a heading to a letter for emphasis or clarity.

With apologies to Aristotle, who said the same of the classic drama, every business letter should have a beginning, a middle and an end. Your letter should state its business at the outset and draw a suitable conclusion at the finish. If you are given to courtesies at the beginning and end of your letters, keep them brief if they are hypocritical; or if they are elaborate, keep them sincere.

If you are replying to someone, it is conventional to say, 'Thank you for your letter of...' and the date. A specific and detailed letter can often carry an underlined heading, following the greeting but over the text, which instantly conveys the topic following.

Style and content

People sometimes talk about style as if it were a mysterious and insurmountable barrier to their progress. Forget about it. Good style is invisible. Your aim is to inform and instruct, and language is like a lot of other commodities: you need neither too little nor too much. Too little, and the job is not adequately prepared; too much, and the words obscure the real message.

Business letters traditionally suffer from too much language. Verbiage and pomposity arose when elaboration was confused with importance. Times have changed, and manners are generally less pretentious now – though human nature doesn't change that much. Business correspondence is still shot through with the subtle stigmata of status. Just remember the basics – be brief, be clear, be courteous.

Be sensitive to the impact of allegations and accusations you may make. If you receive an outrageous but groundless communication, dismiss it lightly – indeed, ignore it.

Occasionally one stumbles across extremely litigious individuals who are both hypersensitive and aggressive. You may not appreciate this until you get a solicitor's letter saying that your last letter implied his client's integrity was in question or his business of no substance and this was a damaging statement etc. In which case you may choose to apologise for any misunderstanding but demonstrate that your letter was an exact reply in no way exceeding the facts, in response to an offensive letter in the first instance...

If you write a letter under circumstances of dispute and it may be referred to a solicitor and either cited in court or taken as a definite statement of your position, head the text WITHOUT PREJUDICE. If you are the complainant, be patient, persistent and extremely clear.

Functional and specialised letters

Most of the specimen letters supplied in this book are specialised, dedicated to particular functions in particular company departments.

Functionalism may or may not be the enemy of beauty – it's an old architectural debate. Your letters are doubtless not designed as monuments for posterity. If they work, never mind the beauty.

Specialised letters entail their own technical terms. We are taught to avoid jargon, but don't – go for it! Jargon talks its own language to the specialist, and your aim is to get through to people. What you should avoid is not jargon as such, but the cliché – the boring over-used phrase, the meaningless exaggeration, the dreary insincerity. Jargon easily slips into cliché, especially with cult language and buzz words. So try not to write in terms of 'entering a profitability mode' or 'facing a dismissal situation', unless you enjoy it and hope your reader does too.

Specialised business letters demand professionalism: expertise and accuracy in handling the information involved. Familiarity with the technicalities or the arithmetic may be only a starting point: before you write your letter consider what selection, structure and judgement you will apply to the data.

Fax and computer

In the last few years offices have been revolutionised by the arrival of the fax and the affordable desk-top computer. Most of the letters in this book can (or should) be sent by fax in the right circumstances. Many of them, tidied up to suit your circumstances, can be keyed into a computer file to be printed out on demand, individualised either to a specific addressee or merged with a mailing list of names and addresses.

Your individual touch

From time to time, out of the repetitive dull trivia of business correspondence, there leaps forth a bright spark of colour. Be as functional as you have to be, but leave room for quality to show. Let your own turn of phrase have its way. The textbooks say, never be frivolous, as if they were afraid of a crack appearing in a façade of iron control. On the contrary, be humorous, be good-natured. It will work wonders with those unknown human beings you correspond with. Most of them, after all, laugh and cry and experience life like you. Most of them appreciate a little quality entering their day.

So do your job well, and with that finer energy you've got stored away, throw in something extra. It's nice to go home with that sense of satisfaction. It's nice when someone writes back to you saying: I enjoyed your letter.

Part 2:

The Letters

Abusive letters

You occasionally receive abusive letters from impatient persons angered by real or imagined grievances, or from eccentrics. Let it be a sign of your inner quality – not to mention the quality of your business – that you never write abusively. There are excellent ways of expressing unpalatable facts and strong opinions, and of replying to abuse. If you have to engage in a fraught correspondence, avoid bad language, threats and insinuations. By all means use irony as a weapon, although it will most likely be lost on an angry or obsessive correspondent. See also: LITIGIOUS letters.

If you receive an abusive letter, the best course may be to ignore it. If a reply is required because, for example, the correspondent is making a claim against you which you consider unjustified, reply patiently, factually and courteously.

Dear Mr Scrapper   [Date]

Thank you for your letter of...

We are unable to entertain your claim for commission and expenses as we did not authorise you to represent our company in the first instance. Please see again our letter to you of...declining your services.

This correspondence is now at an end.

Acceptances

Acceptance of invitation to business or social function

Out of good form you should reply to invitations whether you are going or not, particularly if RSVP (please reply) is indicated on the corner. You reply formally to formal invitations, informally to informal ones. Don't bother to reply to those cards inviting you to exhibitions, demonstrations etc, which are really direct mail shots, unless, of course, you genuinely want to go and earn a glass of champagne in your thirst for knowledge.

For acceptances of formal invitations, use one sentence in the middle of a plain sheet of paper; no dear sirs or yours etc. Remember *Black Tie* means dinner jacket, *White Tie* means tails (evening dress), and with weddings you may need to make enquiries as to whether you wear morning suit and topper.

If you want to decline the invitation, see NO THANK YOU letters.

Acceptance of formal invitation

> Mr Edgar Beaver thanks the Directors of Slinky Software Ltd for their kind invitation on Tuesday, 1 July, which he has pleasure in accepting.

Acceptance of informal invitation, or note to a friend supporting the formal letter

> Dear Milo   [Date]
>
> Many thanks for your invitation to the tenth birthday celebrations of Close Thing Fashions Ltd. It seems hardly a day since you boldly and romantically set up shop. I shall be delighted to come along to congratulate you on the past and wish you well for the future.

Acceptance of goods or offer

Acceptance of goods may have strict legal implications and represent a formal commitment on your part to pay for them. At its most informal, acceptance merely indicates that goods have arrived; signing the driver's delivery note is an acceptance. If in a particular situation you are required to write your acceptance of goods, you may be well advised to indicate that you expect them to 'perform' before you are prepared to pay for them. In other words your acceptance is conditional.

Complex projects involving stage completions and progress payments also entail limited statements of quality approval or product acceptance before the project moves on.

Publishers receive manuscripts from authors but only 'accept' those they undertake to publish.

Straightforward acceptance

Dear Mr Binder   [Date]

500 presentation copies of Business Letters book

We confirm that the above consignment of books, bound to our special requirements, has been received in good order.

Our payment will follow on the agreed terms.

Conditional acceptance

Dear —   [Date]

Topwac model E300 photocopier

This is to confirm that this machine has been installed and is in good running order. It is understood that the machine will perform according to your salesperson's assurances, ie will deliver 100 per cent double-sided copying without a significant level (over 2.5 per cent) of jamming or copy quality defects.

We will run the machine for a trial period of one month from today. If the machine works well, we shall be happy to sign a leasing agreement with retrospective effect. If the machine fails to perform as required, we reserve the right to return it to you, paying only for materials consumed and good copies received.

Acknowledgements

Acknowledgement letters should be sent out of courtesy, when detailed replies are not called for, and may be as short as possible. In some cases formal acknowledgements are called for: when the bank sends you a foreign draft, it asks you to sign and return a copy of the covering letter. Acknowledgements should be sent after important documents and cheques have been received, eg an agent's report and remittance, and in response to messages of goodwill.

Notes of acknowledgements should be sent when you cannot immediately send a full reply, perhaps when the key people are absent or when a matter is complex and has to be researched.

Simple acknowledgement of letter, terminating correspondence

Dear — [Date]

We thank you for your letter of 12 July about the proposed laboratory extension, and note your remarks therein.

Acknowledgement to agent or following receipt of funds

Dear — [Date]

We acknowledge with thanks your sales report for the period April–June and your cheque no...for £...being the remittance due in respect of sales for January–March.

Acknowledging a personal message of goodwill

Dear Henry [Date]

Many thanks for your kind note of congratulation. It looks as if promotion really means exposure to more problems! Thanks for all your support in the past. It would be good if we could meet soon.

Acknowledgement promising fuller reply in due course

Dear —   [Date]

Thank you for your letter of 15 August raising the
matter of product liability.

We will write again within 28 days when we have been
able to check and analyse our records.

or

Your letter has been passed to Mr R F Ledger, our
Administration Director, who will reply to you in the
near future.

Order acknowledgement

Every firm has its own range of options and responses at the first
stage of order processing. It may improve your service if you have a
standard acknowledgement form in postcard format. You can
develop your own version of the following.

Redbreast Novelty Co Ltd, Robin Works, Lark Street,
Finchley, TW1T 200

ORDER ACKNOWLEDGEMENT

                                                    [Date]

☐ Thank you for your order ref...
☐ Your order is being processed and will be shipped
   to you on approx...(date).
☐ We cannot process your order as we lack the
   following details:

   ....

☐ We cannot process your order until you settle the
   overdue balance on your account of £...
☐ The following item/s is/are out of stock:

   ....

☐ The following unavailable items are due in stock

---

within... weeks/months and will be shipped to you then automatically unless you instruct otherwise.

☐ The following items are no longer available and we have cancelled your order:

....

☐ Other:

....

With thanks.
Robina Breathless, Customer Service Manager,
Redbreast Novelty Co Ltd
Tel:................. Fax:..................

Acquisitions

When a large company makes a takeover, a battery of accountants and lawyers will be in attendance. But a smaller organisation can buy out another merely with good accounting back-up and a minimum of legal embroilment. An approach by an interested buyer is often made in a personal way and the details elaborated in discussion between the principals of the businesses.

We offer a letter which might be used in modified form at each stage of the takeover process: (a) a proposal outlining possible terms; or (b) confirmation of terms agreed, subject to contract. In either case the letter should be clearly structured, entailing numbered sections and headings. Such letters may well be accompanied by supporting documents and schedules, eg balance sheets, stock lists, contracts, descriptive material etc. An exchange of letters on this basis – that is, a proposal or offer answered by a letter of agreement – could well constitute a contract between the parties. However, a formal contract should normally be drawn up to attend to the detailed provisions and particularly to the respective liabilities of purchaser and vendor, such as in the matter of bad debts or claims arising before the date of transfer.

Note also that the following letter proposes the purchase of assets out of a company, and not the purchase of the company itself.

Letter proposing terms for the acquisition of another business

Dear Peter   [Date]

Purchase of Bogrich Ballast & Binning

This letter sets out a possible [or: the agreed] basis for the purchase by Amnesia & Aphrodisia Associates (referred to as AAA) of certain business assets of Bogrich Ballast & Binning (referred to as BBB).

We are proceeding on the assumption, to be confirmed, that you will retain the actual company, the transaction therefore consisting in the transfer of assets as subsequently defined.

1. AAA will acquire certain business assets and liabilities from BBB for a consideration based on the net value of the assets transferred, plus a royalty paid for a period of five years calculated on profit performance in that period.

2. The transfer date for the transaction will be 30 June 19...

3. The book values of the assets concerned will be established as at the transfer date by a joint audit.

4. The cash consideration will be paid at the transfer date, subject to any subsequent adjustment required when the audit is finalised.

5. BBB's business assets/liabilities to be acquired by AAA comprise the following, each item to be supported by a corresponding schedule:
   5.1 Stock and finished goods.
   5.2 Work in progress and raw materials.
   5.3 Certain fixed assets.
   5.4 Trade debtors.
   5.5 Trade creditors.
   5.6 Industrial properties, rights and contracts, including:
     – rights to the unrestricted use of BBB business names;

> - BBB patents, copyrights and industrial properties;
> - supply contracts being as yet unfulfilled purchase orders;
> - sale contracts being as yet unfulfilled customer orders;
> - contracts with authors designers consultants subcontractors or other sources of expertise;
> - contracts or licences whereby rights have been granted to third parties
>
> 5.7 Sales and accounting records, promotional material, catalogue information, customer lists etc.
>
> 6. A royalty payment of 10 per cent of net pre-tax profits will be payable for five years on a quarterly basis, the first payment falling due three months after the transfer date.
>
> I hope the above provides a basis for agreement. I will give you a ring on Monday to discuss arrangements for the audit, and will have a draft contract drawn up next week for us to consider further.
>
> With best wishes

Advertising

Letter to candidate agency inviting a proposal for a campaign

Could be done by phone equally well, or letter could be sent in confirmation of phone call.

> Dear Tarquin   [Date]
>
> We are inviting presentations from a shortlist of three agencies for the contract for the 1994/95 press advertising campaign for our MOGGO sleepwear product line.
>
> We admired your recent promotion for Dampartz Lingerie and your approach may well correspond with our own ideas.
>
> Could you give me a ring to let me know if you are interested and to have a preliminary chat? If we are to think of working together I should like to arrange a full briefing meeting before the end of the month.

Letter accompanying ad copy for display in trade press

Address it to advertising manager at the publication in question.

Dear Sherry   [Date]

ORDER

I enclose marked-up copy for a quarter-page display ad in *Nightwear Gazette*.

1. Please set and proof ASAP.
2. We plan to run six insertions monthly July to year-end.
3. Please advise on availability of a good regular position facing text.
4. Please confirm series rate.
5. If second colour available, especially pre-Christmas, please advise.
6. Please note we have supplied overlays for the response coding on the order coupon which should run in sequence, ie NG94/1 on the first ad to appear etc.

Let me know if there are any queries.

Agents and distributors

Agents and distributors are here treated as overseas independent organisations appointed to promote and sell your products. The usual distinction is that agents do not carry stock but receive a commission on orders generated, while distributors carry stock and retain a percentage of sales revenue. It is also common for the exporter to send goods to the distributor on consignment. In a further arrangement, goods are sold by a commission agent in a given territory, who is paid an agreed percentage by the principal after the customer has paid.

The following letters cover various different arrangements. They may also be adapted for inland/regional use. Naturally specific definitions, product descriptions, marketing needs, percentages and commissions are determined by you.

Letter seeking potential agent or distributor

Dear Sirs   [Date]

We wish to appoint an exclusive agent for our Textbook Division in the following territories...

Stock will be held locally. We would prefer a buy-firm agreement, but would consider consignment terms.

We enclose preliminary information about the product division in question. We provide detailed support for our agencies, including regular advance product information and shared promotional material.

If you are interested, could you kindly send us your proposals for handling this product line, covering the following matters:

– other companies represented;
– commercial and financial references;
– summary of market conditions for the product line;
– your organisation, local coverage and promotional activities;
– three-year sales outlook for our products;
– your suggested terms of agreement.

We look forward to hearing from you and to discussing possible terms in more detail.

With best wishes.

Yours faithfully

Letter of agreement to agent or distributor confirming terms for exclusive agency on buy-firm basis

Dear —

This is to confirm the agency agreement between ourselves as principal (A) and yourselves as agent (B) on the following terms:

1. A appoints B on an exclusive basis for a period of

three years starting on 1 January 1994 in the territories of:...

2. B shall buy from A at a discount of 45 per cent off the list price, payable at 90 days following date of invoice. Shipment shall be by surface freight at B's expense.

3. B shall maintain adequate local stocks and adequate storage facilities.

4. B shall promote the product both by direct mail and by personal representation, creating local editions of the annual catalogue and special leaflets from time to time.

5. B shall remit quarterly sales reports by title and quarterly summaries of sales activity.

6. A shall provide B with advance product information, with monthly forward publication schedules, and with (one) free sample of...for office and display purposes.

7. A shall provide artwork or film of promotional material for the agent's use.

8. This agreement shall run for three years minimum and thereafter may be terminated by either party with three months' notice, or may be terminated at any time by either party at shorter notice in the event of material default or insolvency.

I enclose a duplicate of this letter for you to sign and return.

With best wishes.

Signed ....Signed ....

(Principal) ....(Agent)................................

Date: ....Date: ....

Letter of agreement to agent or distributor providing for sending stock on consignment

Dear —

This is to confirm the distributor agreement between ourselves as principal (A) and yourselves as distributor (B) on the following terms:

1. B shall act as A's exclusive representative in the territories of:... for the product lines of:...

2. B shall maintain adequate facilities for storage of stock, order processing and despatch. B shall also maintain adequate stock levels and shall promote and sell the product.

3. The stock shall be consigned by A to B and shall remain A's property until sold. B shall hold the stock insured to the extent of its replacement cost. B shall bear the shipping cost.

4. B shall provide quarterly sales figures and an annual inventory count. Payment in respect of each quarter's sales is to be made by the end of the following quarter, B remitting...per cent of net invoiced revenue.

5. B shall set the local selling price.

6. A shall provide advance product information and specimen material as agreed.

7. A warrants to B that the product is not libellous/obscene/defective and indemnifies B against any such claim.

8. This agreement shall last for two years and thereafter may be terminated at three months' notice by either party, or at shorter notice in the event of a gross breach.

We look forward to receiving your agreement, and enclose a duplicate of this letter for your signature and return.

Yours truly

Signed ....Signed ....

(Principal) ....(Distributor)...........................

Date: ....Date: ....

Letter terminating agency

An optional paragraph is offered if poor performance is the reason.

Dear —   [Date]

Agency agreement – termination notice

This is to give you three months' notice, under our agreement dated..., that we wish to terminate your agency with effect as at ...

[*Optional paragraph*] We have been dissatisfied with your performance during the past year and our letters of .../... give details of declining sales and late remittances.

We have made alternative local arrangements and have instructed our local freight handling agents Messrs...& Co to remove all remaining stock and promotional materials from your premises on ... It is our wish to bring that date forward if possible.

Could you kindly send us an inventory report as at ... and your sales report for the first quarter.

Agreements

A letter of agreement simply states what has been or what is to be agreed between the parties. An acknowledging letter from the other party, or the signatures of both parties on the main letter or a copy of it, have the force of a contract. We refer you to other formal categories of letter in this book including ACQUISITIONS and AGENTS AND DISTRIBUTORS.

If the issue at stake is at all complex, the letter should be structured under *heads of agreement* - ie the clauses to be agreed upon.

A simple letter of agreement to a local distributor

> Dear Mr Wratt [Date]
>
> This is to confirm that we allow you to use the following phrase incorporating our SQUIRREL registered trademark: 'Distributors of SQUIRREL Nuts 'n' Raisins', in letters 12 inches high on your six delivery vans.

Preliminary structure for a more complex letter of agreement

The headings are examples of what might comprise such a letter.

> Dear Harry [Date]
>
> Commercial relationship between Cat Crispies Co and Dog's Dinner Ltd
>
> In order to clarify our thoughts following our discussion I am setting out draft heads of agreement defining the planned relationship between your company (CC) and ours (DD).
>
> 1. Relationship. CC and DD will collaborate in the joint venture 'Pets' Paradise' described in our memorandum of...
> 2. Financial plan ...
> 3. Respective roles of partners ...
> 4. Time-scale ...
> 5. Right to outside work ...
> 6. Definition of net profit ...
> 7. Right to appoint project manager ...
> 8. Cancellation and buy-out options ...
>
> Please let me have your thoughts on this outline. We can then prepare a draft agreement.
>
> With best wishes

Angry letters

If you write an angry letter, it is usually the better course not to post it immediately, but to look at it again next day when you have cooled off. You may find that you don't feel as strongly, the matter appears in a different perspective and you can rewrite the letter more coolly.

As a general rule, if you feel offended or taken for a ride or had your time wasted, you should try to express your anger in dignified language. There are situations where annoyance is legitimate and can be expressed. Suppose you have ordered goods which arrive late and poorly made, but for various reasons you have to live with it and use the material or send it on to your customer. You feel that your time and money have been exploited and your own good reputation is at risk. You might write as follows.

Dear —   [Date]

I am writing to express in the strongest terms our dissatisfaction and disappointment with the ... recently ordered and received from you.

We have detailed separately the delays/defects/etc associated with this order.

I am both surprised and angry that our patience and goodwill have been exploited to an unacceptable extent, with our advance payments and technical support along the way counting for very little when the pressure was on, and with personal assurances from yourself/your senior managers not worth the paper they were written on.

But remember to stay detached, even if you feel furious. Ask yourself: what's in it for us? There is no point in berating somebody and even less in expressing your anger (even if feigned for the purpose of the letter) if you are never going to work with the people again. On the other hand, if matey is your only supplier of furry nuts and bolts, it doesn't make sense to cut off your nose to spite your face. Send him a letter expressing disappointment but in such a way that he'll pull his socks up next time.

See also STRONG letters.

Apology

It depends what you're apologising for, but mostly the principle is the same: you swallow your pride, bare your breast and say you're sorry, even if you're not. Sometimes you have to apologise in the face of legal pressure, as when, knowingly or otherwise, you have injured or offended a third party.

Apology to offended customer, possibly after a complaint

Dear —   [Date]

I am writing to offer the company's sincere apology for the embarrassment caused to you in our store the other day. This event was far removed from our usual standards of courtesy and the member of staff who was rude to you also expresses his regret.

I have asked the store manager to send you a small item with our compliments in the hope of making some amends.

Apology to a competitor to avert possible libel action

Note heading 'Without Prejudice' and the measures taken.

Dear —   [Date]

Without Prejudice

Thank you for your letter of...drawing our attention to the implications of our advertising copy in the press advertisement 'Win through with Winox etc'.

We have taken advice on this matter and write to express our unreserved apology for any implications damaging to your interests, any such implications having been, we assure you, quite unintentional and only perceived with hindsight.

We have withdrawn the advertisement in question from all press bookings.

We are certainly prepared to send an explanatory statement to the trade press on the lines you request, but suggest that such action would merely give public exposure to an issue currently visible only to our two organisations.

Apology for having to cancel an appointment

Dear Mr Corcoran   [Date]

My apologies for having to cancel our meeting yesterday. I am afraid an urgent matter came up which I could not avoid. I will be in touch to arrange another date in the near future.

Apology giving plausible reasons when you actually forgot an appointment

Dear Mr Herbert   [Date]

I am writing to offer heartfelt apologies for missing our appointment yesterday. I had a family emergency, and had to drop everything. All is well now and I am sorry I could not get in touch with you. I will telephone to arrange a new meeting.

Apology for missing a meeting with a friend

Dear Algy   [Date]

A thousand apologies for appearing to forget you yesterday. The truth is I was on my way up from Southampton when a large seagull smashed through the Volvo's windscreen. It was only hours later when I was still being tended by a State Registered Nurse that I realised I should have phoned. Will be in touch.

Apology used as evasion of meeting you don't want. Poor Geoff Smith

---

Dear Mr —   [Date]

So sorry I had to cancel our meeting at short notice, but urgent company business came up. May I suggest, as I am fully committed at present and have to go abroad as well, that you write to me with your proposals.

Yours sincerely

PS. For a quicker response write not to me but to our sales director, Geoff Smith.

Applications

A job application letter should get you past the first hurdle – on to the shortlist and into the interview. To do this it has to give off an air of quality. Such letters are usually accompanied by a *curriculum vitae*.

If you know the name of the personnel manager or person doing the recruiting, write personally, with 'Yours sincerely'. The covering letter should be short and should not repeat, other than to highlight, information given in the CV. Some employers like the covering letter to be handwritten, as the handwriting is informative; this applies more at the clerical than at managerial level. The CV should be impeccably presented.

Application for an advertised post

Dear...   [Date]

I should like to be considered for the post of...currently advertised in the...

I enclose a CV which gives full details of my qualifications and career to date. The following are the main points supporting my application:

For the last three years I have been in charge of...at

Teazle Corporation. During that time the department's work-force has increased by...and productivity by...My specific responsibilities have included...

Although my present working relationships are good, I am eager to develop my career and am looking for more scope and challenge in my work.

I am familiar with your company as a consumer and from reading the business press. I would be grateful if I could come to see you to discuss the opportunity in person.

We do not favour the sort of application letter which reads, 'Hey there! I'm 28, unmarried, male with a doctorate in cybernetics and an O level in common sense, and I could do great things for your company. Why don't you interview me and find out?' You scribble: Thanks but no thanks, on this one. Sales departments sometimes love people like this but that is their problem.

Appointment letters

Generally speaking letters of appointment and dismissal should be formal in tone. A more friendly and colloquial tone may be reserved for letters of congratulation or condolence.

Letter confirming a candidate's appointment

See also OFFERS. Some appointments may be conditional upon performance and subject to a later review.

Dear —   [Date]

I am delighted to confirm your appointment as...following our recent discussions. The post carries a job specification, a copy of which is enclosed for you to retain.

We agreed that you would start on 1 September. The initial salary is £..., to be reviewed after six months.

Working hours, holiday entitlement and pension

provision are set out in the enclosed company staff notes.

May I wish you a rewarding and enjoyable career with our company.

A more formal approach would be to issue the new employee with a Statement of Terms and Conditions of Employment as they relate to him. The Statement would cover the following matters and copies would be kept by both the employee and the employer.

- Name
- Date of engagement
- Title and duties
- Salary, method of payment
- Expenses or allowances
- Period of notice on either side for termination of employment
- Signed by employee
- (Date)

- Provisions relating to:
  - sickness or injury payments
  - pension or life assurance benefits
  - holidays
  - health and safety at work
  - redress of grievances
  - disciplinary procedures
- Signed for employer
- (Date)

Appraisal

Appraisal normally signifies staff appraisal, namely a periodic assessment carried out by department heads and personnel managers and reported on internally in memo form. However, you may be asked to write an appraisal of, say, a competitor's marketing performance. As ever, the structure of your letter is all-important. It flows from the headings. And the most important single section is the final one: your conclusions.

Dear Charles [Date]

<u>Appraisal of WOPPA product launch</u>

The following are the main features of this competitor's performance in relation to our own market position.

1. Product concept. WOPPA is beamed aggressively at the C2/D housewife sectors whereas our own project X has B-segment appeal as well as C1/C2 and should sustain the planned price premium.

2. Pricing...

3. Timing...

4. TV presentation...

5. Packaging...

6. Budget...

7. Conclusions/recommendations:
   (a) Our product concept is...
   (b) Our packaging should convey...
   (c) Our timing should be geared to...

I will be glad to discuss these points in more detail.

Attachments

We all gather attachments as we go through life, and some business letters are no exception. Use attachments to your letter rather than make the letter an unwieldy length by trying to include a report or a proposal in the letter format.

For example, if you are writing to somebody with a complex business proposal, divide the proposal up into bits to make it manageable and send it with a short covering letter saying that you enclose the proposal organised as follows:

Attachment A.	Financial summary
Attachment B.	Marketing territories
Attachment C.	Product development
Attachment D.	Return on investment

See also COVERING LETTERS, PROPOSALS

Audit

A number of letters of a formal nature are required in connection with the statutory annual audit of a company's accounts.

In the first instance the firm of auditors may receive a letter of engagement from the employing company although, where there is a long-standing relationship between the parties, the instructions regarding the audit may be renewed and discussed less formally. The letter of engagement may be written by the company accountant or by one of the directors. Alternatively it may be written by the auditors to confirm instructions received. According to the textbooks the engagement letter should invite, as an essential feature of the audit, a critical review of the client's systems of internal control; the letter may also indicate that all aspects of the business, not only financial, are open to the auditor's scrutiny. Each year particular areas of internal control, such as stock-taking procedures, may be reviewed in turn. A standard form of engagement letter is provided for auditors by the Institute of Chartered Accountants.

The client is required to write a letter to his bank instructing them to make information available to the auditors.

The Manager
...Bank   [Date]

Dear Sir

We hereby authorise you to disclose the audit information required by our auditors, Messrs...

We wish this opportunity to be continued until we countermand it.

Yours faithfully

Director

In some cases the auditors require a director of the company to write a 'letter of representation' to vouch for information which the auditors may have been unable to ascertain. The letter of representation can be seen as a way for the auditor to cover himself for any uncertainties in the audit by ensuring that management takes responsibility for them. The letter of representation may be drafted by the auditors for signature by the company. The following is an example:

Dear Sirs   [Date]

<u>Annual audit for year ending 30 June 19...</u>

We confirm that to the best of our knowledge the information given below is correct and in accordance with the requirements of the relevant Companies Acts as amended.

1. Stock valuation. The following valuation was reached:

$$\begin{array}{ll}
& \pounds \\
\text{Raw materials} & \dots \\
\text{Work in progress} & \dots \\
\text{Finished goods} & \underline{\dots} \\
& \underline{\underline{\dots}}
\end{array}$$

This valuation is based on the following considerations:
(a) raw materials are valued at cost written down to net realisable value where applicable;
(b) work in progress is valued at cost of materials plus direct labour;
(c) finished goods are valued at materials cost plus direct and indirect cost allocations, subject to appropriate writedowns over one year old.

2. Freehold properties. These were valued in March 19... by Bricks, Mortar and Co, Chartered Surveyors, at £...

3. Bad debts. The provision of £...set aside for default among overseas trade debtors is considered adequate.

4. Contingent liabilities. There were no contingent or contractual liabilities entered into but not accounted for at the audit date.

Yours faithfully

(Signed)
Director

A separate inventory letter is sometimes required where a company's stock is of a specialised nature or geographically much dispersed; or where the method of valuation is esoteric. A director is required to set out the method of ascertaining stock quantities and values.

Finally, it is common for the auditors at the conclusion of an audit to set out in a formal letter to the client, called a management letter, weaknesses found in the systems of internal control, with proposals for remedial action. Such letters can, of course, be extremely complex; the following is a short example of a management letter.

The Directors
Aberrant Trading Co Ltd   [Date]

Dear Sirs

Annual audit for year ending 30 June 19...

Following your audit for the above period, we should like to bring to your attention certain points which came to light in the course of the audit. We have discussed some of these matters with appropriate members of your staff and understand that corrective action is being taken.

1. Sales ledger
   In some instances unpaid pro-forma invoices had been posted in the sales ledger as debtors.

2. Petty cash
   We were unable to verify all petty cash expenditure through the absence of a daily record.

3. Order processing
   There is inadequate provision for checking customer credit status before orders are passed for fulfilment, leading to unnecessary bad debts.

4. Stock control
   (a) The requisition system for complimentaries or samples for the sales force is informal or non-existent and had led to unaccounted-for stock discrepancies.

(b) There should be a back-up system to verify the storekeeper's stock movement records.

We trust that the above matters, where they are not already in hand, will be rectified without delay. It is not, of course, our function to determine what supervisory and control systems you should employ, but we are happy to advise on such matters should you require further assistance.

Yours faithfully

(For firm of auditors)

Bank correspondence

If you know your bank manager personally (as indeed you should) and if you are writing to discuss a particular matter with him, write to him by name, Dear Mr...and end Yours sincerely. Otherwise, if you are merely sending instructions or doing routine business, write to The Manager, Dear Sir, Yours faithfully. Most bank transactions require your written confirmation. Address your letter to the appropriate bank department: the Foreign Department for overseas currency transactions; the Securities Department for investment matters; the Trustee Department for lodging your will and for the administration of estates.

Routine instruction to bank

The Manager
...Bank plc   [Date]

Dear Sir

Please transfer £5,000 from our current a/c no...to our deposit a/c no...Could you please advise current interest rates for your various classes of deposit account.

With thanks.

Yours faithfully

Request for foreign currency draft to pay overseas account

The Manager
Foreign Department   [Date]
...Bank plc

Dear Sir

Please draw a US dollar draft for $5,000 in favour of:

Festive Supply Co Inc
948 West 86th Street
New York, NY 10088
USA

Please send the draft to this office for my attention as soon as possible, debiting the sterling equivalent to our current a/c no...

With thanks.

Yours faithfully

When you do have to write personally to your bank manager, it is often to provide an account of activities and prospects of your business, in support of your request for continued borrowing facilities or a business development loan. Classically, the bank manager asks you for a sales forecast and cash flow analysis, and sometimes for a profit and loss statement. You provide the cash flow information in schedule form, with a strong covering letter picking out the salient features on your business horizon - the tricky ones as well as the good ones. Remember the old adage: give the bad news all at once, the good news slowly. This applies particularly to bank managers.

Letter to bank manager supporting negotiation of borrowing facility

Dear Mr Gladly   [Date]

Following your recent request I now enclose our cash flow forecast for 19...

The schedule shows sales by month, fixed and variable costs, and monthly and cumulative cash balances.

My comments on our prospects for the year are as follows:

1. Sales forecast. We are looking for around 20 per cent growth on the present year. We are putting a lot into promotion at present, which should generate strong sales in the early months. We can then take in our stride a quieter summer period and will not have to depend on something 'turning up' at the end of the year.

2. Cost increases. Variable costs are pro rata to sales with economies of scale in good months. Fixed costs are bumped up in the second half, as we expect a rent increase and will have to take on one or two more people.

3. Profitability. Over the full year we expect to show 8 per cent net profit on sales. There may be an opportunity for pricing action in the second half which would improve this performance.

4. Cash flow. By the year end our cash flow marginally improves over the current position. But we do go through a period early on of financing additional stock and waiting for cash to flow back out of increased debtors. We will need your support during that phase and perhaps we could discuss the provision required in more detail.

5. Conclusion. I see the forecast period as one of steady development while maintaining profitability. The cash call early in the year will turn positive by the year's end and the company's net asset position will improve satisfactorily.

Yours sincerely

	J	F	M	A	M	J	J	A	S	O	N	D	Total

CONFIDENTIAL
ENCLOSURE: Cash flow forecast for 19...
...Company Ltd   [Date]

	J F M A M J J A S O N D Total
Sales Less credits, commissions Net sales	
New debtors Total debtors Cash inflow	

Variable (or
  volume) costs
Fixed costs
  payroll
  overhead
Total costs	

Cash inflow/
  outflow
Cumulative cash
  position	

Cash opening position: Closing position:

Bank references

A bank reference is written by a bank in response to your enquiry about the financial status of one of its customers, frequently when you need to decide whether to supply goods on credit, but also when you need assurances about a firm's substance if, for example, you are about to grant a lease to a tenant.

Banks couch their references in mysterious terms, partly because they are not prepared to disclose confidential details about their clients, and partly because they decline liability for the consequences of any action you may take based on their information. In fact you may do better by asking your bank manager to have a word with his opposite number at the other bank. Bank references are *not* a guarantee of payment, as credit controllers know to their cost. See also TRADE REFERENCES, which can be more useful.

Letter taking up a bank reference

Note the invitation to telephone, in case information can be hinted at informally but not in writing.

Dear Sir   [Date]

Your bank has been given to us as a reference by Mr S Moorhen, commercial director of Wagtail Piling Systems, who have placed a substantial order with us. We would appreciate your indication whether this company would be good for meeting invoices totalling £7,500 over the next three months.

Please telephone me if that is more convenient for you.

Thank you for your help.

A bank's reply – positive

Dear Sir

In answer to your query, Wagtail Piling Systems would be good for the amount indicated at the present time.

A bank's reply – negative

Dear Sir

In answer to your enquiry about Wagtail Piling Systems, we are unable to vouch for the information you require.

Begging letters

You probably haven't seen many *real* begging letters, unless you have won the pools. You probably don't send many, either.

Occasionally, you receive a letter running like this:

Dear Mr Peters (it was Bill wasn't it)

You won't remember me but we once worked in the same office back in the old days at Fawcett Street. You probably remember the affair of the paper pellets and Miss Penfold. What a laugh that was. I wonder what became of her. Well I went off to better myself but life hasn't been too kind including an unfortunate episode in which I was deprived of my liberty and unjustly I maintain. Now I am doing my best to make my wife a proud and happy woman again although our kiddie has been v. unsettled. I was wondering whether there might be any kind of a Position going at your organisation which would suit.

Yours in hope, T.F. Smith

If you are a busy, important person you don't reply. If you have a spark of compassion you reply one way or another. You could even ask your personnel people to see what could be done, reflecting that you never know but you might pick up one of those staple employees that way. Or if you want to fend the person off you write as follows:

Dear TF   [Date]

I was interested and touched to get your letter, and sorry to hear of your hard times.

I have checked around our departments and there is just nothing going at the moment.

Life can appear unjust and I can only suggest that you stay close to your family and give your kiddie lots of attention. Perhaps things will take a turn for the better.

See also CHARITY APPEALS

Business proposals see Proposals

Cancellations

Whether you can cancel with impunity or not depends what you're cancelling. If you cancel an order or project for which the supplier has invested in work and materials, you will be charged for them. In some circumstances you will be asked — or sued — to pay a contribution to loss of profit too.

But most cancellations can be short and sweet.

Cancelling an appointment

Courtesy or close acquaintance, of course, may demand a fuller explanation or a gentler turn of phrase. See APOLOGY.

Dear —   [Date]

May I cancel my appointment with you on...at...as I will be away [or as the meeting was rendered unnecessary by our recent phone conversation].

Cancelling a date with a friend

Dear Toby   [Date]

Sorry, but I have to cancel our presentation meeting with you fixed for Thursday.

Our people have made their decision and it looks as if we won't be working with you this year.

Let us have a lunch some time anyway.

Cancelling an order where there is no commitment to a contract

---

Gentlemen: [Date]

Our order ref...date...for...

We CANCEL this order.

Yours truly

However, there may be good reasons for cancelling an order.

Dear —   [Date]

Our order ref...

We regret that we are obliged to cancel this order. Timely delivery was of the essence, and you have now advised us that production is running four weeks in arrears.

We find that our own commitments are jeopardised by this lateness, and must make other arrangements.

Could you kindly acknowledge this letter.

Catalogues

Sometimes it makes a nice touch to print a letter inside the front cover of your new catalogue, or on a separate sheet and tucked inside. 'A letter from the managing director', or 'From the sales director', it might be headed. It begins 'Dear Customer'.

Consumer goods/mail order oriented letter

Adapt it for your products. For industrial or professional products, a less euphoric tone is called for.

Dear Customer

Welcome to our new catalogue!

This is our seventh annual catalogue and to celebrate that lucky number we've prepared some new and fascinating collections for you.

Right at the front you'll find the season's new lines – straight from the designer, they've just come into stock. We think there are some wonderful shapes and colours in there, inspired by this year's Italian look.

Next we have a section of specials and speciality items. You'll find the strangest ideas in there and you'll wonder, 'Why didn't anybody think of that before?' Well... we just did, and here it is for you.

The third section contains our perennials – those trusty old numbers you seem to keep coming back for, or you know a friend who wants one.

And finally, the bargain basement section, where we can let older lines and surplus stocks go at really ridiculous prices.

Happy hunting! Oh, and – thank you. You're our customer, and we appreciate you. Each year we try to come up with bright, attractive ideas, and each year we hope you come back and try some of them out. And remember – don't hesitate to write to me personally with your own suggestions. I'll reply to you on the dot.

Cordially yours

Richard Benson
Sales Director

Change of address

If you move premises or change your phone number you can send an ordinary change of address card. But you may prefer to write to suppliers and customers. You naturally inform the trade press too.

You might also think of writing to key customers or suppliers if you take on a new sales director or manager who will be the interface

Dear —

CHANGE OF ADDRESS

The growth of our business has prompted us to move to new premises. With effect from 1 April 19.. our address will be:

The Green House
Garden Place
Aylesbury
Bucks HP00 1NK
Tel (0333) 333333 Fax (0333) 333344

The changeover will allow us to improve the quality of our service significantly as well as continue our rapid rate of expansion. We greatly value our business relationship with you and the friendly contacts between our firms.

With best wishes

between you and outside companies. You could also send word to the New Appointments feature in your trade mag.

Charity appeals

Doubtless you receive plenty of these. If you can, you put a fiver in them and send them back. The company can make charitable donations, so if you have the authority you can send company money. Whether political donations are charitable is another matter.

You may have to write an appeal letter – perhaps your firm's staff contribute to a good cause, or you are on a local fund-raising committee.

Dear friend   [Date]

Make a real gesture of goodwill!

Do you remember what wonderful results your efforts achieved last year when everyone combined forces for our local Children in Need day? So many people said later that their work and their contributions gave them a real feeling of satisfaction and doing something of value.

Next month on 15 October, we are going to put on another special Day of Help to raise funds for a field treatment unit for the...Overseas Medical Appeal. Our target is £...! and with everybody's help we'll jolly well reach it.

You can help us in three ways:

- Send us a cash or cheque donation, payable to...

- Send unwanted items to the Grand Auction. Phone up Graham Purling on...and he and his helpers will collect your gifts.

- Come along to the Jubilee Room at 11.00 on the 15th! Meet your friends, have a cup of coffee and join in a variety of fund-raising fun.

I look forward to seeing you there. Remember – most of us in this community live very comfortably. Surely we have a little something to spare to give to others. Don't let us down...don't let yourself down.

Yours sincerely

Geoffrey Monketon
Charity Appeal Chairman

Chasing letters

See also CREDIT CONTROL for chasing up unpaid invoices. You may need to chase up projects and orders awaited from suppliers. In some cases the telephone and/or a personal visit are the best means of pressuring a tardy supplier. Otherwise you have to write. Send key letters by fax for immediate impact.

As with all chasing mechanisms, successive letters (if necessary) should increase the pressure. Don't make idle threats. Try to encourage a positive response and positive thinking from the person you have a problem with, rather than blustering and bullying into evasive manoeuvres. After all, you are normally stuck with a supplier once the order is placed; cancelling and starting again may take longer than chasing and waiting.

Progress control chasing letter

All good progress chasers keep tabs ahead of the due date to keep in contact with the supplier, and so that probable slippage, if any, can be estimated.

Dear Alf   [Date]

Our order ref...for...

I am checking my schedule and note that delivery of this order is due one month today.

Can you kindly confirm to me by phone or in a written note that the delivery date will be kept? It is, of course, essential for our own operating and contractual commitments that there is no delay.

I would like to get an idea of how the project is progressing when we talk on the phone. You know that we are available to discuss and work through any snags that may arise.

May I hear from you by return?

First chasing letter after non-delivery – could be sent by fax

---

Dear Alfie   [Date]

Our order ref...for...

As of today's date our order placed with you on...is now seven days overdue for delivery.

Could you kindly get in touch immediately to let us know the circumstances behind the delay and give us a firm revised date. I will ring you tomorrow if I have not heard from you by phone or fax before then.

Second chasing letter after non-delivery – soft approach

Dear Alfikins [Date]

Late delivery – our order ref...

We are still awaiting an answer from you to our earlier letter(s) of...

Please let us have a firm revised delivery date for this order.

We will take a sympathetic view of any difficulties and would like to work with you to achieve early completion and delivery. Please let me know what the circumstances and the outlook are, and I will visit you in the next few days to help get the project back on the tracks.

Further chasing letter after non-delivery – hard approach

Dear Alfred [Date]

Late delivery – our order ref...

Following our earlier correspondence chasing this order, we hereby give notice that we require the order to be delivered to our premises by the 31st of this month.

We have failed to secure a revised delivery date from you, or such as you have given have been broken, and we have no choice but to impose a date on you.

It is, of course, essential to our own contractual commitments that we should have these goods delivered on time.

We consider that your actions now place you in breach of contract, but we are happy to accept the goods and pay the agreed price as long as our stipulated delivery deadline is met.

If by any chance it is not met, we shall have no choice but to consider cancelling the order, to assess if our own commercial interests have been damaged by your delay, and whether we would be well advised to place future similar orders elsewhere.

Could you kindly acknowledge that you have received and understood this letter.

Christmas

Add Christmas greetings to your letters before Christmas. It spreads goodwill among all the Bob Cratchits.

And don't bother to have posh Christmas cards printed for the firm. Go out and buy some charity cards. You can always have them overprinted or stickered if you can barely scrawl your signature.

Circulars

The term 'circular letter' is rather dismissive and the circular as a rule is treated with scant attention.

However, many businesses depend keenly upon successful deployment of mail order and direct mail techniques, which use carefully prepared packages of promotional material. See DIRECT MAIL.

The circular is usually a single-shot leaflet, often delivered through letter boxes for domestic promotions and local offers. The leaflet usually incorporates a response coupon and may also feature an attention-grabbing letter.

Sales letter appearing on circular for down-market local promotion

The aim of the letter is to be glanced at, rather than read and considered, and to provoke action - ie return of the coupon. This will provide a lead for a sales call.

Dear Householder

The scale of your problem...!

Why don't you sit down and have a nice cup of tea while you read this? – but don't look in the kettle! All that furry scale building up round the element. It gets worse every day, doesn't it? You'll need a new element one of these days – or a new kettle, more likely.

And those dreadful tidemarks round the basins! That stain where the tap was dripping! And the discoloured lavatory bowl – not even bleach seems to get it clean for long.

And if you could see inside your central heating system! Well – you'd be horrified. If you've had a heating system in for ten years, some of the piping and radiators could be so furred up as to cut their capacity by a half. Imagine what that does to your heating efficiency – and your fuel bills.

Madam, we hand it to you – you've got scale! But you'd be better off without it. Your problem is that you live in a HARD WATER AREA. So-called hard water carries minute mineral traces floating in it, and these minerals build up deposits inside pipes and appliances.

Help is at hand! Install a DINOSAUR Water Softener and the dreadful scale build-up will stop. Indeed, much of the scale will gradually dissolve away in the newly softened water.

Just sign the reply-paid coupon below, add your address and post it today. No stamp required. Our local soft water consultant will call and advise you on the most economical softener unit to solve your scale problems. The cost? Less than you think – and you can pay in easy instalments.

One thing is certain – when you post that coupon off, you're going to finish up saving money, and improving your quality of life. Well done!

Sally Lewis
Customer Relations

Collection see *Credit control*

Complaints, making

This section deals with letters when *you* are doing the complaining. The next entry provides letters for when you are at the receiving end.

Complaints arise from poor quality, poor performance and poor service. In some cases, if a product arrives damaged or doesn't work, you may have grounds for sending it back. In other cases your only recourse is to complain and try to get the offender to raise his standards. Don't hesitate to complain. Sometimes you haven't the energy to make an issue of small things. But business people need reminders when they let their quality slip. Don't worry. You know your customers don't let you off if you give bad service, and some of them can be quite nasty.

Complaint about article damaged on receipt

Dear Sirs [Date]

Re: our order ref...for office desk

This desk was delivered yesterday and upon examining it we find it to be severely scratched across the top. We cannot accept it in this state and should be obliged if you would immediately deliver a replacement and take this one away.

Complaint about poor performance

Dear Sirs [Date]

Re: delivery van regd no M14 SMA

We took delivery of this vehicle yesterday and on closer examination our driver has reported a leak of hydraulic fluid and a deflated spare tyre.

Could you rectify these matters before the weekend as the vehicle is urgently required for delivery work?

I have instructed that our cheque to you be held until the vehicle is considered A1.

I take a poor view of this situation as you customarily assure us that you give your vehicles a pre-delivery check.

Complaint about poor service and discourtesy

R T Ffoulks, Esq
Managing Director
Ridgeway Tooling Company   [Date]

Dear Mr Ffoulks

I write to complain about the poor service we have recently received from your company and the discourteous treatment meted out to one of our junior staff.

1. On 20 October we placed our order no...for a batch of 100 AA size castors to one of our particular specifications. We were given a job no...and a completion date of 7 December.

2. On 30 November we got our junior progress chaser to ring to get confirmation of delivery. She was treated to various remarks like 'What order?' and 'It's Postles Furniture pestering us again', and 'Why don't you...etc, darling'. She had to give up the attempt in distress.

3. On 1 December our production manager spoke to his opposite number Bill Trant and was told there was no record of such an order and why didn't we sort ourselves out.

Well, I am afraid the boot is on the other foot. It is now 8 December and still no delivery from you. I am shocked that your organisation can indulge not only in incompetence but in personal discourtesy. I am also shocked that your staff see fit not to take our custom seriously. You need take us for granted no more. I am reluctant to break a relationship going back 35 years to your father's time but I will gladly look for an alternative supplier who is able to work to acceptable standards of efficient service and personal politeness.

Yours sincerely

Complaints, answering

Dealing with complaints is a common enough necessity. We all make mistakes and we all have difficult customers. Handling complaints usually comes under the larger responsibility of CUSTOMER SERVICE.

The general rules in answering complaints are – assuming the complaint is justified – be courteous, apologise, make amends, don't lose the customer. The challenge is to turn the situation around so that you win over a previously aggrieved individual by the quality of your response.

Let us imagine that we were at the receiving end of the letters of complaint on the preceding pages.

Answering complaint about article damaged on receipt

Gentlemen [Date]

Re: your damaged desk

Please accept our apologies for delivering a damaged item. By the time you read this the scratched desk will have been replaced with a mint one. We are remitting 2 per cent off our invoice as a small gesture to compensate for the delay and annoyance you suffered.

Answering complaint about poor performance

Dear Mr — [Date]

New delivery van

I write to apologise for our apparent laxity in preparing this vehicle. The faults you mention were, of course, rectified immediately the following morning.

Our mechanic has shown me his service log and I do believe the hydraulic system was checked over as it should have been. However, it seems possible that the reservoir began to leak on the journey to your premises.

I must confess that the spare tyre seems to have escaped our attention, and regret this oversight.

For all this lapse from grace, I stand by our assurance that you can rely on our high standards of professional maintenance. Our staff share my commitment to quality in our work.

Answering complaint about poor service and discourtesy

Mr G F Postles
Postles Furniture Ltd   [Date]

Dear Mr Postles

I write in answer to your letter about poor service and discourtesy.

I was shocked and mortified to receive your letter. I would have liked to think that I, too, conducted my business to old-fashioned standards of prompt service and good manners. I offer my sincerest apologies.

In a strange way your complaint has done me and our company a service. It was high time for a little stern intervention. I have spoken severely to the lads in that department; they are not a bad lot at heart, a bit lively perhaps. They are sorry to have distressed your young lady and I think they are going to send her a little something. Meanwhile our production manager Bill Trant has had a flea in his ear and is much chastened.

In the circumstances I am not surprised you have cancelled the offending order, but I would just say that we could get that batch of castors out for you by Christmas, should you reconsider.

I would hate the long association between our companies to come to an end. Perhaps after the dust of this exchange has settled you would be prepared to call by on your way home one evening and we could have a drink together. We have an industrial robot system going into the machine shop in the New Year which you may find interesting.

With kind regards.

Yours sincerely

R T Ffoulks

Answering a somewhat abusive complaint

You cannot, of course, say in the letter that every now and then with one unfortunate customer everything that can go wrong, does.

Dear Madam [Date]

I am extremely sorry you have had so much trouble with your order for our book, *Bedside Manners*, with so much delay, and then getting the wrong book, and then being charged incorrectly.

I have checked with our order processing department and they are today sending you the right book at the right price. To express our apologies and goodwill I am sending you herewith a complimentary copy of our booklet, *Fun with Feathers*.

Seeing off a false complaint

Dear Mr Pelwick [Date]

I am sorry to learn that you believe our office computer terminals cause interference on your television set. Please bear in mind that even were this technically conceivable our equipment is not in use in the evening. I must also dismiss your claim that our delivery drivers observe your wife in the bath by standing on their lorries.

I must decline your request for financial compensation and declare this correspondence at an end.

Computer-generated letters

Standard letters or semi-standard letters, such as credit control, customer response or direct mail letters, can be kept in a WP file in the computer and printed out on your stationery in a merge with your database address file of customers, debtors, prospects etc. The profusion of styles and fonts available now combined with high-quality printers means that computer-generated letters no longer look like the dimly printed circular letters of yesteryear.

Unfortunately, the computer doesn't yet write the letter. You have to do that – and proof-read it for errors. Your computer installation software may include a dictionary or spell-check system. It will also probably provide a cardfile facility for storing most used names and addresses.

Examine your business for routine, repetitive or technical correspondence for which master letters can be kept in memory. Accounting and legal offices will be used to working with computer-based formats for financial analysis, contracts, deeds and wills. If you run a sales office, think about putting product descriptions, standard quotation or business proposal texts on file.

Conditions, changes of

You may write an internal letter to an employee to confirm a change in his or her working conditions, in other words a change in job specification. It may represent a promotion, or a containment or sideways move for the problem employee. You should, of course, discuss the changes and agree them in a meeting with the employee first. You should provide a revised job specification – one copy for the employee, one for the company file.

Change of conditions letter – promotion

Dear George   [Date]

I am pleased to set out the changes in your job role following our talk today.

1. As from the 1st of next month you will take over management responsibility for the Despatch Room, with the job title of Despatch Manager.

2. This responsibility entails ensuring smooth despatch operations and maintaining the company's target of two working days for average turn-round between goods leaving Assembly and leaving the premises, and getting the goods safely to their destinations.

3. You will have two packers and two drivers reporting to you and you will be responsible for making sure they have the right skills, good morale and good output.

4. You report to Bill Wright as production manager, and will attend his weekly output meeting to report on the running of the Despatch Room.

5. These job changes represent an increase in responsibility and I am putting through £...per week salary increase as from next month.

Congratulations on this new role – I am sure you will make an excellent job of it.

Change of conditions letter – disguised demotion

Dear Frank   [Date]

Following our talk I would like to give you more specific responsibilities in the order processing area.

Instead of having all orders pass across your desk I am asking Ruby to give them a preliminary sort as they arrive from the post room in the morning.

All orders for Button Division will then come to you for processing so you will be able to specialise in that area.

This way I believe the work of the whole department will run more smoothly and you will, I am sure, make a valuable contribution to it. There will be no salary changes at this time but we will, of course, look closely at the new arrangements when the annual review comes round.

Condolences

Write briefly and sincerely to the bereaved person. If you can say something short and agreeable about the departed one, do so. Remember the aim is to offer consolation and support to the grieving survivor.

Straightforward condolence letter

Dear Mrs —

We were so sorry to hear the sad news of Ernest's death. Our thoughts and prayers go out to you in your loss.

With our kindest remembrances.

Yours sincerely

Condolence letter to the widow of a colleague

Dear Betty

We were all quite shattered to hear your sad news. Letters are an inadequate way of expressing sympathy but we would like you to know how deeply we feel for you.

Edward was a splendid colleague, quite exceptionally loved and admired by everyone. I have received many private letters of tribute which I will send on to you. Those of us who knew him well will miss not only his high degree of professionalism but his frequent humorous asides and way of generating good feeling all around him.

We hope that time will eventually soothe your grief and that the support of your loving family will help to assuage the pain.

The directors join with me in expressing their condolences and sorrow at your great loss.

Condolence upon bereavement after a long illness

Dear —

We were so very sorry to hear your sad news. Even though it was known that Graham was not likely to recover, that cannot have made things any easier for you.

Perhaps there is some consolation now that his suffering is over and you may find peace.

> Please accept our most sincere condolences and deepest sympathy. You have all our support.

Condolence to a mother on the loss of a son, perhaps a junior employee

> Dear Mrs —
>
> We were profoundly shocked to hear of Peter's untimely accident. There can be no worse pain or suffering for parents than to lose a child.
>
> As a colleague Peter was a fine worker and well liked. He will be much missed.
>
> We send our heartfelt sympathy and condolences to you and your husband. If there is anything we can do for you please let us know.

Confirmation

A letter of confirmation is extremely simple. You just write stating that you confirm whatever it is. You may have to spell out a lot of detail after that if, for example, you are confirming an agreement for an operating system.

Confirming an agreement

> Dear —   [Date]
>
> This is to confirm that we have reached the following agreement:
>   1. You will write four quarterly market reports for us of approximately 5,000 words each, examining...etc.
>   2. The reports will be delivered to us on ...
>   3. We will pay four fees, following delivery of ...
>
> I look forward to hearing from you in due course.
>
> Yours sincerely

Confirming an offer of employment

See APPOINTMENT letters and EMPLOYMENT for the details of such a letter.

Dear Mr Upward   [Date]

I am writing to confirm our offer to you of the position of Production Controller. We have already fully discussed the details.

1. Your responsibilities are set out in the accompanying job description.

2. Your starting salary will be £..., to be reviewed at the year end.

3. Holiday entitlements and pension scheme details are set out in the enclosed booklet.

The starting date is 1 June. I understand from our telephone conversation that you intend to accept and I would be glad if you would confirm this as soon as possible. I look forward to having you work with us.

Confirming acceptance of a job offer

Dear Mr Lofty   [Date]

Thank you for your letter of...offering me the post of Production Controller.

I confirm my acceptance of this post and will be free to start, as planned, on 1 June.

I look forward to joining...Company.

Congratulations

Congratulations on promotion

Dear —
Congratulations on your recent advancement! Well
deserved, I may say, and I am sure you will make a
great success of the new job.

Congratulations on appointment

Dear Harvey
Just to congratulate you and wish you well in your new
appointment. That job was crying out for someone with
energy and vision, and I am sure you will be a terrific
success.

Congratulations on marriage between friends

Dear Madge and Charlie
Just to congratulate you both on making respectable
people of each other! Only your friends know how each
of you moped around when the other wasn't there, and
how a strange glow entered your eyes as the loved one
approached. Here's wishing you both many years of
great happiness.

Congratulations on a colleague's marriage

Dear Susan
Congratulations and best wishes to you both from the
old firm. We all spent <u>weeks</u> scouring the town for a
suitable token of our goodwill, and hope the
accompanying package (or its contents) embellishes
your new household. Here, of course, it's business as
usual while some people go off on honeymoon. Have a
wonderful time!

In sectors such as insurance or accounting, an employee who gains a professional qualification is usually due a salary increase, and there may be a standard letter for confirming this and congratulating at the same time. The same principle can be extended to staff who pass technical or institutional grades.

Dear —   [Date]

Congratulations on achieving your...I am/We are delighted that your hard work has been rewarded.

I am also glad to confirm that as a result your salary will be increased to £...with effect from the 1st of next month.

Contracts

See ACCEPTANCES, OFFERS and other letters in this book. Remember that an exchange of letters can constitute a contract, ie an offer or implied offer, and in return an acceptance or implied acceptance. Head your letter 'Subject to contract' if you are discussing a deal but don't want anything you say to be construed as a commitment. It is usually a good idea to keep contracts separate from letters. See AGENTS AND DISTRIBUTORS. Conversely, a simple agreement does not require an elaborate contract or solicitors' fees. Write to your pal and say, it's a deal.

Covering letters

If you have a document, or a book, or some other package to send to someone, it is polite to send it with a covering letter. A covering letter may well be functional as well as polite if you need to explain anything about the accompanying material. See also APPLICATIONS.

Covering letter directing the recipient's attention in a particular way

---

Dear —   [Date]

I enclose our budget estimates for 1995–2000. I would draw your attention particularly to the recommendations in the concluding section.

Covering letter giving explanation of a complex package

Dear —   [Date]

I enclose the dossier of our claim documents for the loss incurred at Chateauvieux. The documents are numbered as follows:

1. Newspaper cutting
2. Police statement
3. Witness statement
4. Schedule of effects involved
5. Garage estimate.

Could you kindly acknowledge safe receipt.

Credit assessment

See also REFUSALS

Requesting status information from new customer

Dear —   [Date]

Thank you for your order ref...

We welcome you as a new customer but regret we do not have enough information at present to extend our usual credit terms. Our credit assessment form is enclosed and we look forward to seeing it completed so that we can review our terms to you. As the form indicates we shall need one trade and one banking reference from you.

Meanwhile we enclose our pro forma invoice and have your order ready for shipment as soon as we receive your payment.

Continuing to refuse credit terms

Dear —   [Date]

We regret we cannot extend our regular credit terms to you as the information made available so far is not sufficient.

We hope that we can reconsider the position in the future if we receive adequate assurances.

Meanwhile we shall be glad to supply you on a pre-payment basis and will send pro-forma invoices when we receive your orders. We look forward to developing our mutual business further.

Credit control

Times have changed. Businesses are often desperate for cash these days and will rapidly apply extreme pressure to force payment from a late debtor. Gone are the days of gentle reminders. If it is you who are late you can find your credit status under question and the prospect of legal recourse against you without all the warning stages of a decade ago.

If you have a small-scale business, try to get paid on the spot. Collect a cheque before the customer leaves your premises, or before you leave his. It saves a letter.

The traditional practice is to have at your disposal a series of more or less standard letters to start sending out when an invoice becomes overdue. The letters start as moderate reminders and escalate in severity and pressure. There are no sure-fire formulae for such letters. All experienced credit controllers have their favourite batches of letters which they know work reasonably well in practice; or else they maintain constant experimentation with new formulae.

The real art of credit control is to assess your risk so you are *not* dependent on letters to get payment out of a bad payer. In the last resort letters don't force a customer to pay, especially if he is overseas or evasive and the debt is too small to justify recovery costs. If a debtor has no money or no intention to pay, you can write until you are blue in the face. Having said that, let's see how you can devise the wording and psychology of your chaser letters to the best effect.

There is one other factor. Niceties of wording are all very well but you are more likely to get paid if you hammer away with frequent, regular letters. Give the debtor no peace and he may pay. Write to him in beauteous tones and what does he care? He doesn't sit down to study your letter for its literary merit. He may be foreign and the nuances will be lost on him anyway. He glances at it. You have a second to make him act, before he screws the letter up and throws it away.

So keep it short. Make it a reminder. Make it speak to him and get under his skin, so he pays up to get rid of this fly buzzing round him.

Credit control procedures also vary according to whether you have relatively few large debtors, or relatively many small ones. In the latter case you have to use standard procedures, and hope they work. We provide a range of letters, from very soft to quite hard. We don't venture into legal action for debt recovery, which is outside our scope. You can buy the services of a collection agency; go for a reputable national and international organisation such as Dun & Bradstreet or the Credit Protection Association. Unpaid debts are referred to the agency after an agreed point such as two months.

The first reminder

This is likely to be a pre-printed letter, accompanied by a statement. All such chasers should be addressed to the purchase or finance department of your debtor, preferably by name to the department head.

Dear —   [Date]

Account no.../Invoice no...

According to our records the above account dated...is now overdue for payment.

The amount owing is £...

We look forward to receiving your payment.

Yours sincerely

M Oregano (Mrs)
Credit Controller

A second standard reminder

Dear — [Date]

Account no.../Invoice no...

May we again remind you that this account is overdue for payment. See copy invoice herewith for your reference.

If the account has already been paid, would you please contact the undersigned who will investigate any discrepancy.

Yours sincerely
TURNER PAGE LTD

M C Drastic
Credit Controller

Further stages should entail personal letters to reach the attention of senior people.

A letter to the chief accountant or finance director

Dear — [Date]

Account no...
Amount £... overdue since...

I write to point out that your company is in arrears with its account to the extent indicated above.

You may be unaware of this, and I would appreciate any explanation if there are special circumstances. Otherwise we expect you to trade with us on the agreed terms, and we look forward to your prompt payment of the amount outstanding.

Another approach to the accounts department, first threatening to revoke, then revoking their credit status.

Dear Sirs [Date]

Account no...
Amount £...overdue since...

We have had no response to our earlier reminders asking for payment of your overdue account.

We will be obliged to cancel your credit status unless we have your cheque in full settlement of the arrears by 31 July.

Dear Sirs [Date]

Account no...

Amount £...in arrears

Since we have not received your cheque in this morning's post, we have withdrawn your trade credit status and your orders currently in the pipeline with us will be processed on a pro-forma basis.

Please settle the overdue account by return. If payment is not received by 1 August we will put a STOP on processing all orders from your company.

Putting a customer on STOP

Address the letter to a senior person so the impact of the action is understood.

Dear — [Date]

Your account... Amount outstanding £...

We regret that you have still not paid your overdue account and as from today we have put a STOP on processing orders from you.

Please make arrangements to pay this account in full so that normal trading may be resumed. If we do not hear from you by 31 August, we will take further measures to recover our debt.

However, you should think twice about resuming normal trading once some debts have been recovered. Keep bad payers on pro forma or curtail their credit status.

Bad payers sometimes send sums on account. Good payers too can have a bad month and send a contribution to the outstanding balance (see also DEFERRED PAYMENT). If you are not prepared to accept partial payment on account, you write as follows. Make sure you bank the cheque, however nominal.

Dear —   [Date]

Account ref... Amount outstanding £...

We have received your cheque for £...in partial settlement of your overdue account.

We appreciate your desire to reduce the amount owing. However, the account remains outside our permitted terms of trade, and we must insist on receiving your further cheque for the balance of £...within seven days.

When you reach the stage of all your letters failing to extract payment, if the customer is in the UK you can instruct a solicitor, or take out small claims proceedings yourself through the County Court. See the textbooks on credit control. Quite often, when a customer doesn't pay and you take legal action you find he was in the process of going bust anyway. The moral is: stop the line of credit early on, when you first smell a rat.

If the customer is overseas, you have a harder job. Sometimes you can put pressure on by writing to the Commercial Counsellor in your Embassy there, and asking him to contact the firm and press it diplomatically, or preferably undiplomatically.

As the card up your sleeve, have a letter to the boss ready, expressing pained disappointment that his accounts department has not sent a cheque. He may, of course, have instructed them not to pay you, but you can only try. Calling into question the honour and integrity of the company has been known to work with overseas firms. Otherwise they pay when they need to order something else from you.

When eventually you run out of road, none of your letters has persuaded the debtor to pay, and you reach the point of legal action, you can inform the debtor as follows:

Dear Sirs   [Date]

Account no... Amount outstanding £...

Despite our reminders and requests for payment over a period of...months, you continue to owe us the amount above.

We are now obliged to take legal action to recover our debt, and you will hear shortly from our representatives.

In some cases, debtors don't pay until they receive a solicitor's letter, which suggests you should put more pressure on sooner.

The alternative course is to invoke the service of one of the collection agencies if you choose to subscribe; the usual course is to buy a book of 'vouchers' which entitles you to so many collection actions. The agencies tend to prefer to be notified sooner rather than later, not unnaturally, in order to have a better chance of collection. The agencies supply their own suggested standard letters.

Remember that time is often of the essence with credit control action. You might communicate some of the preceding messages by telephone because that way you reach the right person and you may get a personal assurance of payment. Or, of course, you send your letter by fax to convey urgency and immediacy.

Credit, letters of

Letters of credit used to be carried by travellers in order to procure funds when abroad. Your bank gave you a letter to present to their correspondent bank in the foreign country. The letter would read 'Please pay the bearer of this letter the sum of £...' The practice was displaced by travellers' cheques, which in turn are giving way to credit cards and international cheque clearance.

The *Irrevocable Letter of Credit* remains in use as a system for providing an overseas supplier with secured payment before he permits shipment of the goods. The 'letter' is an interbank communication. You instruct your bank that funds of £... are available to meet the supplier's invoice. Your bank sends a letter of credit to authorise its correspondent bank to pay the supplier upon sight of the shipping documents. The shipping documents come through to you, the purchaser, while your payment, possibly by a dated bill, is sent to the correspondent bank. With luck the shipment reaches you too.

There are a number of variants on this kind of system for foreign trade payments. Your bank or your shipping and forwarding agent will for the most part handle the exchanges by standard procedures.

Credit references

See BANK REFERENCES and TRADE REFERENCES

Customer service

See also COMPLAINTS and ORDER PROCESSING

Customer service can be just another euphemism for acknowledging orders and deflecting complaints. But we know exactly what customer service ought to be when we are at the receiving end:

- when we want an apology, an explanation or a replacement;
- when we want patience and help to decide on a purchase;
- when we want instructions or adjustments after purchase;
- when we want precise information and not fobbing off.

You know what your customers want – the same as you: civilised treatment. They are surprisingly forgiving and will settle for reasonable service provided it comes with courtesy, goodwill – and information. Be friendly and keep the customers informed. Try to convert a dissatisfied customer into a regular customer.

Sometimes it is quite hard to keep a customer informed when you don't know the answer yourself, such as when an item is coming back into stock. But you can promise to inform the customer when the item does come back into stock, and create a reminder system for doing so.

Answering a customer enquiry

Dear Mrs Fringe   [Date]

Thank you for your enquiry about our leisure products range.

I enclose our current catalogue and order form. You can order from us directly or from the nearest stockist listed in the catalogue.

If you would like to discuss your order or if you have other queries, please get in touch with me or one of my colleagues in Customer Service.

Yours sincerely

Laurence Curtain
Customer Service

Writing to an impatient customer

Dear Mr Baleful   [Date]

I am sorry you have had to write to us a second time about the article you are waiting for.

We did expect it to be back in stock last month having been so informed by our own suppliers – but unfortunately they let us down. We should have written to you to let you know.

We have checked the next delivery, and fully expect to be able to deliver your order by 30 October.

Please accept our apologies for this inconvenience.

Yours sincerely

Writing to a dissatisfied customer

Dear Mr Knightley   [Date]

Your electric pyjamas

I am sorry to hear that your pyjamas do not work, and quite understand the annoyance and anxiety this can cause.

Normally this is a very reliable product, and I can only apologise for the difficulties you have had.

Please return the pyjamas for us to check over, as it has been known for the in-line fuse to blow – fortunately for your safety and peace of mind! If this doesn't do the trick we shall be glad to change them or offer you a choice of our other electrical garments.

Letter to dissatisfied customer, aiming to win more custom in future

Dear Customer   [Date]

Thank you for writing to us to complain about your bad experience with your lawnmower.

We greatly regret you have had such difficulties. Normally the model in question is a reliable one. I can only apologise, supposing that you were unlucky with that particular machine. Please let us know if it still gives trouble and we will contact your local dealer.

May I make a constructive suggestion? We have a new model on the market now, much improved, and only slightly dearer than yours, which you must have bought a little while ago. When you are ready to buy a new machine, we will supply the current model at 25 per cent discount.

We are anxious to show the underlying concern with quality in our business. We would like to keep in touch with you as a valued customer – and eventually, we hope, as a satisfied one.

Decease of colleague

Occasionally you have to notify customers or others of a death in your company. You can send round a duplicated letter such as the following.

Dear friends

It is with much sadness that I have to tell you of the sudden death of John Dell, our sales manager. John made an enormous contribution to the development of the business and we greatly appreciated his sterling character and infinite kindness.

I would appreciate it if for the time being you approached me directly with any matters you would have raised with John. I am concerned to ensure continuity in our service.

Yours sincerely

See also CONDOLENCES

Defamatory letters

You will not, of course, be writing any defamatory letters. Normally defamation, alleged or otherwise, arises in the press when statements are made which the subject objects to. But be careful. You could carelessly make derogatory remarks in a letter to a friend about a mutual acquaintance. You could write, for example:

Did you read about the Pop-up Foods launch last week? I see Rodney Mulheap was involved in that as well; he must pick up commissions on both sides...

Be discreet. You can say it in the pub instead of putting it in writing. Copies of letters pop up in strange places.

An act of defamation brings another person into hatred, ridicule or contempt. Defamation can occur in the form of slander, when the injury is done verbally and therefore may pass quickly and unrecorded; or it may occur as libel, that is, in written form or, curiously, on TV or radio, which media are presumably regarded as permanent in their effect. Bear in mind that the fact that a statement is true does not prevent it from being defamatory.

In certain circumstances you can make defamatory statements about a person but enjoy what is called 'qualified privilege'. In business, for example, you may be called upon to make uncomplimentary statements in a reference or otherwise about the performance of a member of staff; or perhaps in an exchange of letters about the behaviour of a third party. Be as discreet as you can. Bear in mind also that malicious intent removes your 'qualified privilege'.

You are allowed, as newspaper editors reflect daily, to make otherwise defamatory remarks in the course of 'fair comment on a matter of public interest'. If you are at the receiving end of a communication you consider defamatory, the best course is to ignore it. You risk looking ridiculous if you insist on saying 'Oh, no, I'm not!' in front of an audience. 'Oh, yes, you are!' comes back the chorus.

Deferred payment

Circumstances arise when you cannot meet all your month-end commitments or cannot repay an overdraft at the agreed time. It is better to write first, rather than wait to be chased, to show you are ahead of the game. The assurances you can make to your creditors depend, of course, on whether you do expect more funds next month, or not. The aim of the letter is to secure their agreement without worrying them.

Letter requesting more time to pay when you expect your situation to improve

Write to the chief accountant or credit control manager.

Dear —   [Date]

Your invoice no...for £...

This payment falls due at the end of this month.

I am writing to ask if we can agree a special arrangement with you for late payment. We recently secured increased overseas orders but at the cost of a temporarily extended cash flow. We expect certain sizeable orders to be paid for within the next two months and ask if we may defer payment of your account from 31 August to 31 October.

Our debtors are sound prospects and the question is purely one of timing. Thereafter we will, of course, revert to your normal terms of trading and indeed would look for some increase in our level of business with you. I am sure you will be able to accommodate us through this bridging period, and thank you for your help.

Letter requesting more time to pay when sales have fallen off, cash flow has fallen off, and you have a problem

Again, address the letter to a senior person who can take decisions to alleviate pressure on you, rather than to the credit control clerk whose job is to tidy up his or her list of outstanding accounts at all costs. Part payment plus the promise of regular instalments add some substance to the letter.

Dear —   [Date]

Your invoice no...for £2,342.50

This account is now due, and I am writing to ask you to grant us a slightly extended period in which to complete the payment.

Our cash flow has entered upon a seasonal flat spot, aggravated by dull market conditions. To be pessimistic, it may be several months before we see a strong upturn. However, you will be reassured to know that our business has a sound net asset position with underlying strengths in its product line. We have taken immediate action to counter adverse trading conditions by reducing our expenditure, and will see a more positive cash flow out of stocks over the next few months.

I would ask that we be allowed to pay your account by four monthly remittances of £500, with a final adjustment in the fifth month. I enclose our initial cheque for £500 now.

It would be difficult for us to make a more substantial commitment at the moment, and I trust you will be able to accept our proposal as the quickest way of clearing your account.

Letter to bank asking to defer repayment of loan

You can add the explanatory detail of either of the preceding letters if appropriate.

Dear Sir   [Date]

Repayment of Business Development Loan

We are, of course, making monthly payments to you of £... to repay the BDL.

This month and next month we are under temporary cash pressure resulting from tight trading conditions. May I ask you to arrange a three-month moratorium in our repayments in order to give us some leeway.

This would mean final repayment of the loan at a date three months later than that currently scheduled. Our underlying net asset position remains unchanged and I am happy to endorse my director's guarantee for the loan should the new timing require this.

With thanks

Yours faithfully

A moratorium is a period of grace, which creditors will sometimes allow a hard-pressed company, in order to get their money later rather than not at all. Enforcing payment in such circumstances might well only have the effect of enforcing liquidation.

A letter requesting a moratorium

Dear —   [Date]

As you know times have been difficult for us recently, and we remain under considerable pressure, though I trust temporarily. At the present moment we cannot meet our commitments and I am afraid your account must remain unpaid at least for the time being. I am meeting urgently with our bank and with other parties to see how the situation can be turned round. It is, of course, our wish to continue trading if at all possible and to pay outstanding accounts in full. I believe there is a good prospect of this. May I ask you to bear with us patiently for a while as any precipitate action leading to premature liquidation would be in neither our nor your own best interest. I will be in touch with you again within the month to keep you informed of developments.

A response to a request for a moratorium

Dear —   [Date]

We note your request to postpone payment of our account.

We are willing to allow two months' grace, on condition that the account is paid without fail within seven days following 30 April.

Or the following, which is more cautious:

Dear —   [Date]

We note your request to postpone payment of our account.

We would like more specific information before agreeing to your request, and suggest we arrange a meeting in the near future, with a view to our receiving firm assurances of payment, possibly with the support of your bank or by a series of post-dated cheques.

Delays

Advising customer of expected delay in delivery

Dear —   [Date]

Your order ref...

We have suffered delivery delays from our own

suppliers, and have no choice but to put back the delivery date for this order by one month from 1 March to 1 April.

We are most reluctant to take this step as we are anxious to maintain a top level of performance in fulfilling your orders. Unfortunately the cause of this matter lies beyond our control.

Apologising for late delivery

Dear —   [Date]

Your order ref...

I am writing to apologise for our late delivery of this order.

We normally pride ourselves on our good service, but in this case the project proved more complex and time-consuming than we had allowed for. We greatly regret any inconvenience and hope the quality of the material makes up for a degree of lateness.

Delicate letters

This kind of letter is better accomplished verbally if possible. For example: telling someone he has a drink problem and needs help; or telling his wife her husband has a drink problem. Telling a person you are firing them because of their dishonesty; telling a mother her son has been caught stealing. Telling one of your friends to pull his socks up in some way. In a way, writing the letter is the easy part; taking the decision to act can be harder.

Dropping a hint to a colleague with a drink problem

Spelling out the problem would be done face-to-face.

Dear Charlie

We don't seem to have bumped into each other lately, so I am dropping you a note. I would like us to have a chat urgently. Word is reaching me that your work is really suffering, and I think if we recognised the fact, we could do something about it. Trust my friendship – this note is off the record. Why not drop in around 5 o'clock either tomorrow evening or the next day?

Breaking news that will be unwelcome

Telling (in no uncertain terms) a mother or wife who insists on knowing why her son or husband has been dismissed.

Dear Mrs Furlong

Strictly speaking we are not obliged nor even entitled to inform anyone other than the employee concerned of the reasons for his dismissal. However, since you press us and mention a possible appeal, to save you or Tony unnecessary further effort or distress, the facts are as follows.

Tony was dismissed for bad timekeeping and poor work.

He was found to be absent without notice or sufficient explanation on six afternoons in May and June and three in July; and late returning from lunch on ten other occasions in that period. His supervisor found reason to speak to him several times on account of work unfinished or badly finished or, on one occasion, because of a number of orders found hidden away in a drawer. He received written warnings on 31 May and 30 June without apparent effect, and we therefore asked him to leave the company as at 31 July.

Dropping a hint to a colleague that he should look for another job

Dear Charlie

Just a note off the record to say let's have a drink one evening soon. I am a bit concerned by the look of things in your department. We haven't been seeing the right figures coming up and morale generally is suffering. I think, frankly, you are under a lot of pressure in an uncongenial atmosphere. Times change, and you have accomplishments you could exert in other fields than this. Let's talk about the best thing to do.

Delivery

A letter seeking delivery instructions

Sent when goods are nearing readiness for despatch; best sent by fax.

Dear — [Date]

Your order ref...

Your order will be ready for despatch as arranged during the week beginning Monday...

Please let us have full instructions for delivery, including any special packing requirements, mode of transportation and preferred shipper.

If you have no preference our regular shippers and forwarders are Messrs...and we will arrange for them to pack and send your goods.

Note that for the complexities of import/export shipping and documentation you should refer to a specialised textbook on export procedures - or place matters in the hands of your shipper and forwarder.

Letter confirming a delivery date

Dear — [Date]

<u>Your order ref...</u>

We are able to confirm the delivery date for this order. The consignment is booked to leave our premises on 15 December by Beeline Transit Services and it should reach your Fagnall Lane depot not later than 18 December.

Letter revising a delivery date you can't keep

See also DELAYS. Delete inapplicable reasons.

Dear — [Date]

<u>Your order ref...</u>

Because of unavoidable difficulties with our own suppliers/with a defective machine, which has now been repaired/in the industrial relations area/ arising from complexities in the order, we regret that we cannot keep the scheduled delivery date of 7 December. We are writing to advise you with maximum advance notice that the delivery date is now revised to 17 December. We have taken strenuous measures after considerable difficulties to maintain delivery to you after minimal delay.

Direct mail

The direct mail package usually consists of:

- a selling letter;
- a descriptive leaflet;
- an order coupon.

The precise configuration of the package varies from industry to industry or indeed from one practitioner to the next. The letter may be a separate letter or part of the leaflet. The order form may be a cut-out coupon or a reply-paid postcard. Some mailing shots, especially those for large colourful countryside companions or books of the world's mysteries that every household needs, include special offers, premium gifts, competitions and extremely elaborate, well-nigh incomprehensible folding brochures and sets of rules. The complexity and cost of the package are (presumably) geared to the scale of the operation and effective response it generates.

The direct mail letter (see also CIRCULARS) is structured to achieve four successive aims:

- catch the reader's attention;
- awaken conscious product need (or at any rate, desire);
- indicate availability of product;
- clinch ordering action.

Mailings are, of course, directed towards specialised lists of people likely to be interested in the proposition by virtue of their job, memberships, subscriptions etc.

A direct mail letter to sell a book like this one

Dear Manager [Date]

The answer to those business correspondence headaches

Were you dreaming, or did you imagine a letter arrived offering to solve a business problem which wastes hours of your time and has you uttering low groans of despair? That pile of business correspondence, lying in wait every morning. Those awful letters you have to churn out, make them effective, make them smart – but make them readable too. And not take all day over it. How are you going to manage that, manager?

You weren't dreaming. The letter arrived. You are reading it. You are awake here and now reading this.

There is a book called *Readymade Business Letters That Get Results*. It contains hundreds of specimen letters dealing with all the common business situations. Acknowledgements, agents, apologies, applications, appraisals, bank references, complaints, condolences, credit control, dismissal, employment, enquiries, estimates... – it goes on and on. Abusive letters, fan letters, love letters. Thank you letters, no thank you letters. It's all there. Even tells you how to plan your letter, write nicely and what to say, with affectionate – sorry, with best wishes at the end.

You're not dreaming. This book exists. It exists in a warehouse. Fill in the order coupon and people will send it to you...then your old business letters had better look out. And your headaches and low groans.

Thanks for your order!

With affectionate – sorry, with best wishes.

Jenny Allnutt
Direct Sales Consultant

Dismissal

The dismissal of an employee can only be undertaken on well-defined grounds and must normally be preceded by at least one warning (see also WARNING letters). The area of performance or poor performance of a job can be vague and further clouded by personal animosity. So grounds for dismissal have to be specific, if possible measured against the company's general terms of employment (such as working hours) or against the individual's job specification. The dismissal arises in a sense from the employee's breaking of his contract, or his implied contract, of employment. He should understand and if possible accept the reasons for his dismissal, otherwise there is the possibility that he will seek redress for unfair dismissal. If an employee is a member of a trade union, you should contact the local union representative before the dismissal and explain the circumstances.

The amount of notice served on an employee depends on his legal rights and on the contract of employment - a week, a month, or longer. There is a legal minimum period of notice for long-serving staff. For example, staff with more than two years' service are entitled to one week's notice for each year of service up to a maximum of 12 weeks' notice after 12 years' service or more. Make sure you are familiar with the formal requirements – they are more important than the way the letter is written. Summary dismissal, although unusual, may still be made when a gross offence occurs, such as theft or vandalism, or if it would be embarrassing or undesirable for the person to stick around; his pay for his notice period is sent on to him.

Letter giving employee a month's notice

Note that such letters do not come out of the blue; they confirm a 'discussion'. The same letter could be modified to give a week's notice.

Dear —   [Date]

This is to confirm that you will leave the company with effect one month from now, ie on Friday, 27 June.

This action follows on our warning letters to you dated 10 March and 30 April about poor work. Unfortunately we have seen no improvement. Some of our specific instances for complaint were noted in our discussion.*

I am sorry to part company in this way and wish you well for the future.

---

* This suggests that you keep the documented reasons for dismissal on file for a time in case there is any come-back.

Letter to a more senior employee after agreeing to 'part company'

Dear Henry   [Date]

We agreed at our meeting that you would be leaving the company at the expiry of three months' notice, ie by 30 September.

In fact, I think it would be counterproductive for both of us if you stay with us in these circumstances. I suggest you tidy your affairs and leave as soon as is convenient for you. Let me know when this will be and the company will of course give you a cheque for three months' pay 'in lieu of notice'.

Letter effecting summary dismissal

Dear —   [Date]

This is to give you notice of dismissal with immediate effect, following the discovery that you have been taking food and cash from the canteen for the last three months.

We have decided not to call the police in, although a criminal offence was involved, in the hope that this will enable you to make a fresh start.

We enclose a cheque for one week's wages in lieu of notice.

Note. This letter 'writes off' any funds stolen from the canteen, rather than confuse matters by, for example, withholding any wages due. The offender could be asked to make restitution as a separate issue.

The question of payment in lieu of notice can be handled in different ways. Since the payment is tax free, it works out as a bonus and reward which are often undeserved. You may prefer this accidental generosity in order to make a clean break. A manager may prefer, unless the person has committed a gross misdemeanour, to make him or her work out notice, but not necessarily doing the same job; thus, a salesman would hand in his car and work a month in the office. Perhaps it depends whether you have to work alongside him.

Distribution

See also AGENTS AND DISTRIBUTORS

An offer to undertake distribution of a third party's product line

The letter below envisages a marketing service rather than merely a storage/order fulfilment system. In most cases, but not necessarily all, the product line will be imported, chosen because it fits with existing product and extends the sales volume passing over existing overheads.

Operating details, percentages etc can be adjusted according to circumstances.

Gentlemen:

Distribution and marketing service

We are interested in undertaking the distribution of your...product line and would like to present the following proposal for your consideration.

We feel that the...product line is insufficiently represented in our market area. There is a good fit between your line and our existing products which cover, as you know, an extensive range, including...We have a substantial sales budget and run an effective marketing system involving:

- catalogues and price-lists twice yearly;
- monthly mail shots of subject lists and special selections, mailing quantities...;
- trade visits by representatives;
- participation in trade shows.

We suggest the following outline of terms for a distribution agreement;

- Distributor's market area: UK and Western Europe;
- Product supplied on consignment;
- Distributor remits 40 per cent of net receipts on a quarterly basis;
- Distributor undertakes storage, order fulfilment, and a full marketing service;
- Distributor has reasonable pricing discretion;
- Distributor maintains stock control system and reorders from time to time;
- Agreement runs for three years initially.

If you are interested in our proposal in principle, we shall be glad to send a draft distributor agreement and to discuss terms in more detail.

We shall be glad to send trade references which will speak for our marketing resources.

We are confident that the proposed distributorship will be to our mutual benefit, and look forward to hearing from you.

Yours truly

Distributors see **Agents and distributors**

Employment, offers of

Typical letter of appointment/offer of employment for junior/middle level office post

This letter contains a brief job description. A more complex job description would be on a separate document. See also APPOINTMENT letters.

Dear Mrs/Miss —   [Date]

Following your interview I am happy to offer you the post of secretary in the sales department. I gather you plan to accept the post, and will be free to join us after the end of the month.

Responsibilities of this post include:

— typing letters for sales manager and two reps when they're in;
— organising and maintaining orderly files;
— answering telephone enquiries with enough general knowledge of the company's products to help the customer or pass the query on to the right person;
— updating the product information file and organising the printing of new leaflets and price-lists;
— assisting the sales manager with presentations, trade shows and promotional activity.

Your starting salary will be £...per annum, payable monthly in arrears and subject to review each December. In the event of termination by either side, a month's notice must be given.

Working hours are 9–5 Monday–Friday with an hour free from 1 to 2. Luncheon vouchers are available. Holiday entitlement in a full year is four weeks, not more than two weeks to be taken at any one time. This year your pro-rata entitlement will be two weeks.

After two years you will have the option of joining the company's pension scheme.

Once you have a sound knowledge of the company's products there will be opportunities for training and increased responsibility.

I am delighted you are joining us and welcome you to Cortex Ceiling Joists Ltd. We hope you will have a successful career with us, and look forward to seeing you on Monday, 1 July.

Offer of employment subject to probationary period

In such a case references would have been taken up before the offer was made.

Dear —   [Date]

We are glad to offer you the post of check-out assistant with effect from Monday, 1 July.

The position is subject to a probationary period of one month in which you will undergo two weeks' training followed by a trial period. Following the successful outcome of the probationary period, you will be offered a permanent post.

During the first month you will be paid a weekly wage of £...After the post is confirmed you will go on to a monthly salary.

We look forward to seeing you on Monday, 1 July at 9.00 am.

Offer of a more senior appointment

Note the hint of an 'out' after six months if it doesn't work.

Dear Mary [Date]

Following our recent discussions I am delighted to offer you the job of marketing director.

I am impressed by your track record and am sure you can contribute a great deal to getting our business moving along the lines we discussed.

As you know we want to move fast now and your specific remit is get our sales off their present level to the £5m mark by the year 2000. The first task will be to prepare a comprehensive mid-term business plan.

The detailed terms of employment, company conditions and so on are in the booklet you already have.

We propose an initial salary of £...with a performance review at the year-end. If things have gone well we will be happy to discuss a profit-linked incentive of the sort you were asking about.

We are looking forward to working with you. Come and see me first thing when you arrive on the 25th.

Enquiries, making

Try to find out which department or which person you should address your enquiry to. If in doubt address it to the Sales Department or Customer Service Department. Answers to enquiries are given in the next section. See also CUSTOMER SERVICE. The simplest way to enquire about product information or to request a catalogue is to ring up and ask.

Asking about a job

Address to the Personnel Manager. Find out his name by ringing up first.

Dear Mr Kindly [Date]

I should like to apply for a position with your firm if and when there is a suitable vacancy.

I am interested in the marketing or sales assistant/market research area. I am 27, female, with relevant job experience and good references; please see enclosed CV.

If there are no vacancies at present, perhaps I could ask you to be kind enough to send me an application form to complete and return so that you will have my full credentials ready on file for another occasion.

Enquiring whether a manufacturer or machine shop will make something special for you

Dear — [Date]

Special tool rack

We need a purpose-built section of tool rack for our workshop, and understand that you are able to fabricate one-off items to customer requirements.

The enclosed drawing gives the dimensions and other specifications of the piece.

Could you indicate as soon as possible whether in principle you could make this item? We could then work out the details so you could prepare an estimate.

Asking for estimate

Dear — [Date]

Request for estimate

We are interested in ordering 500 copies of *Readymade Business Letters That Get Results* bound in hand-tooled green goatskin leather with embossed front and gilt lettering on spine, as a business gift for our distributors. See specimen copy/specification and dimensions enclosed. Could you kindly send us an estimate.

Enquiries, answering

Be as informative, pleasant, and positive as you can.

Answering an enquiry about product availability

Dear Mrs Marmot   [Date]

Availability of synthetic fur bedlinen

Thank you for your enquiry.

This line is still available, but subject to three weeks' delivery from the date an order is received.

Recommended retail price is £99 per set with 30 per cent trade discount, carriage paid. We would quote improved terms for stock orders for five or more sets.

Regretting that a product is not available

Offer a substitute instead.

Dear Madam   [Date]

Kingsize rolling pin

We regret this line is out of stock and the manufacturers tell us they have no plans to make more.

We would be happy to sell you the medium-size rolling pin, price £6.95 in best ashwood. I am sure this excellent pin will meet all your marital needs.

If you care to post a cheque we will send the medium-size rolling pin post free.

On second thoughts, leave the joke out. Or leave it till you have her cheque.

Answering a customer enquiry and creating a sales lead

Dear Sir Arthur   [Date]

Many thanks for your enquiry about insulation. We sell a variety of heat-preserving systems for the home, from cheap to reasonable. They all save you money in the long run.

I think you had in mind rolls of 'Loftrap' insulating material for your loft at £...per roll.

I suggest my colleague Bill Glass calls round to measure up your tower and see how many rolls you need, or anything else. He's extremely helpful.

Remember that most enquiries can be viewed as sales opportunities, so send information, set up a meeting, convert that lead! See also FOLLOW-UPS.

Dear Mr Vole   [Date]

Thank you for your enquiry about our FERRET underfloor heating system.

I enclose descriptive literature and details of our do-it-yourself installation system and easy payments plan. I have asked our sales engineer, Rupert Stote, to call on you in a few days' time to show you how the FERRET system would fit into your home.

Thank you again. You'll be glad you installed FERRET – it gets the warmth everywhere under your feet!

Yours sincerely

Rhoda Weazle
Customer Service

Answering a query about company policy

Dear —   [Date]

Thank you for your enquiry about our company
recruitment policy.

Our objective is to operate as an 'equal opportunity
employer', that is to seek staff in the light of their skills
and personality without regard to their sex or ethnic
origin. We do in fact give special attention to all
individuals who may have been denied educational or
professional opportunities hitherto but who could
contribute to making this company a successful
business and social community.

Estimates

Estimates, especially complex ones which break down into sub-esti-
mates, are often provided on standard forms or in standard formats
according to the industry concerned. Printers' estimates for book
production follow a particular structure and are frequently set out on
estimate forms with small print on the verso establishing conditions
under which the work is carried out. Such estimates not only break
the job down into its component stages, each with a price, but indicate the cost of extending the print run within a given range. See also
QUOTATIONS.

The following are straightforward estimates incorporated in letter
form. If you send out a lot of estimates you should number them and
file the copies accordingly in order to tie up the subsequent job with
its quotation.

A simple estimate

But don't forget the courteous conclusion.

Dear —   [Date]

Estimate no 86/41 – Garden Shed

Following your enquiry, we quote as follows for a

---

garden shed in cedar 12′ × 8′ with pitched roof and one standard window plus one extra window.

Price delivered and erected £...

We would be able to deliver within five working days of receiving your order, and look forward to hearing from you.

A more complex estimate

There may well be extensive small print at the foot or on the back of the estimate relating to terms of trade, responsibility for property, liability to the other party etc.

Dear —   [Date]

Estimate for catalogue

Further to your letter of...and our subsequent discussion, our estimate for this job is as follows:

To production of catalogue, A5 page size, extent 64pp plus cover saddlestitched, paper text 80 gsm cartridge, cover one sided Koptex 240 gsm, black on white throughout, full colour on outside cover. Allow for 40 line illustrations in text. Cover artwork provided, we to make separations. Quote for 20,000 run with 5,000 run-on. Prices valid for 60 days from above date.

	For 20,000	Per 5,000 run-on
	£	£
Typesetting	......	–
Make-up	......	–
Paper (text)	......	......
Printing	......	–
Cover separations	......	......
paper	......	......
printing	......	......
Binding and trimming	......	......
TOTALS	......	......

> We confirm that if we receive marked-up text from you by 30 September we can proof by 21 October with 7 days turnround for proof corrections and achieve delivery by 15 November as required.
>
> We look forward to hearing from you.

Euphemistic letters

See also DELICATE letters

Promoting an employee sideways instead of upwards

> Dear Freddy [Date]
>
> I have given a lot of thought to organisational questions in anticipation of our annual review. I feel that some of our products are not getting enough managerial attention. At the same time I would like to put more focus on your own responsibilities so you can have the satisfaction of working towards specific goals. Putting these factors together, I am recommending that you be designated Operations Director, Kleenwipe Division, with product, market and budgetary responsibility for this important sector of ours. We will discuss the details. We will be able to shade your salary upwards in recognition of this change of horizons. Good wishes for the new challenge.

Explaining why a disliked advertising presentation was rejected

> Dear Olly [Date]
>
> Many thanks for the pains you took the other day. We have, however, decided not to go along with your interesting proposals as they seem to be too innovative for our present market policy of consolidation.

Writing a reference for someone you are glad to see the back of (see References)

> Dear Sir [Date]
>
> I am happy to supply a reference for Mr Albert Burdock, who has worked with us for a number of years, and has proved to be a careful and conscientious employee. With the experience that he now has, he is anxious to try for an opportunity elsewhere and we think that you will find him an excellent worker.

Telling the chairman what you think of the painting he has bought for the lobby

> Dear Chairman
>
> I wanted to congratulate you on your latest acquisition – hanging in the lobby. A lot of people have remarked on its vibrancy and hypnotic effect. May it exert the first of these powers on us and the second on our competitors.

Export/Import

Export (and import) correspondence is often considered difficult and complex. There are specialised books on this topic alone. But the problems really arise from one factor: the often elaborate procedures for shipping and payment between different nations. This main factor may be complicated by a diversity of language, though English is largely accepted as a worldwide trading language.

The complexities of international trade lie therefore in the procedures, and not in the correspondence. The procedures for shipment and payment are largely taken care of by your shipping and forwarding agent, and your bank (see also SHIPPERS). In so-called 'export-import' correspondence, you are only carrying out the same basic business operations:

Export	Import
• Looking for markets	• Looking for suppliers
• Selling to the markets	• Negotiating on estimates and prices
• Dealing with agents and distributors	• Setting up markets and distribution this end
• Shipping goods	• Shipping goods
• Dealing with customs clearance	• Dealing with customs clearance
• Sending invoices, collecting money	• Paying invoices

Setting it out like this tends to demystify what is going on. You can write straightforward, functional letters, only making allowance for your reader's (possibly) limited command of English. See also FOREIGN CORRESPONDENCE. If possible, correspond by fax. Otherwise, or even so, prepare for a lengthy process. The telephone will come in useful and a personal visit may eventually be needed.

If you are starting from scratch, ask your bank to write to its correspondent bank(s) in the territory asking their local people to send you a shortlist of potential distributors, or suppliers. You can also send a similar letter to the commercial section of your local Embassy. You can research the matter at home, by checking with the BOTB Export Representative Service, the library, the trade press, the professional institutions – and by asking colleagues in other companies. See also correspondence under AGENTS AND DISTRIBUTORS.

Letter to bank asking for list of potential distributors in a given territory

The Manager, Foreign Department
...Bank plc   [Date]

Dear Sir

Export agents in the Gulf States

We are, as you know, a small company specialising in security systems and alarms for commercial and domestic premises. We want to develop certain overseas markets, in particular certain areas of the

Middle East, and believe this can be done through top-class stock-holding distributors.

However, we have no suitable contacts at present. Could you kindly make enquiries on our behalf with your overseas branches or correspondent banks in the Gulf States, to ask if they can put forward names of potential agents.

Candidates should be established in either the construction or electrical sectors and should, of course, be well regarded.

We will take the correspondence further when we have some names to write to.

Thank you for your help.

Similar letter asking for list of potential suppliers

The Manager, Foreign Department
...Bank plc   [Date]

Dear Sir

Enquiry re: potential suppliers in Far East

We are, as you know, a small business specialising in marketing self-assembly furniture, such as bunk beds and book shelves. Hitherto we have imported most of our stock from suppliers in Eastern Europe. We should now like to look for more economical alternatives, and are interested in seeking estimates from potential suppliers in Taiwan.

We have no contacts there at present. Could you kindly make enquiries on our behalf with your overseas branch or correspondent bank in Taiwan, to ask if they can put forward names of potential suppliers. Candidates should be reliable organisations in popular/low cost furniture manufacture.

We shall take the correspondence further when we have some names to write to.

Thank you for your help.

Fan letters

Here is a kind of fan letter

Dear Prime Minister

May I say, as a small businessman, how very much I agree with your recent remarks about internationalism and the spirit of the twenty-first century. From our modest base we in our company are striving to embody that spirit. For example, it occurs to me to mention that only last month we won a large export order for 1,000 specially carved bulldog walking sticks from North Korea.

Respectfully yours

A Sweetbread
Director
PS. May one ask for a signed photograph?

This letter, although interesting in the light it throws on our overseas trade, may not win you a knighthood. It may attract a reply saying, 'The Prime Minister's secretary thanks you for your kind letter, which was much appreciated', and perhaps the added suggestion that you enter for the Queen's Award for Export Achievement next year.

Here, however, is the sort of fan letter you *should* write. It's called staff appreciation.

Dear Peggy

I believe that at the end of this week you will have been with us for ten years – this is just a note to say well done, and thank you. You've had many compliments you probably don't know about – often callers have remarked to me what a pleasant voice greets them on the switchboard. I always enjoy hearing you down the line, but then I'm your no 1 fan...

All the best.

Fax letters

The fax is the best thing to hit business letters since the typewriter. It combines the immediacy of the phone call with the permanence of the written record. It is ideal for the urgent situation where you have to act immediately and seize an opportunity, eg send a quotation, accept an offer, deliver an ultimatum to a debtor, confirm shipping details, change a specification, redraft a document at long range – or simply send your visitor a map of how to find your office.

In particular the fax has revolutionised relations with overseas customers and to a certain extent has replaced the airmail letter. Now enquiries, quotations and orders can be exchanged within a day. Acceptance of a pro-forma invoice can be confirmed by faxing to the supplier a photocopy of the cheque which is being sent. In many situations faxed documents and faxed signatures are accepted as sufficient for an agreement. In other cases the original documents have to follow by post. Some customers, particularly in certain countries, insist anyway on receiving original invoices.

Many companies use covering sheets for their fax communications, doubtless necessary where many incoming and outgoing faxes are handled by a central point serving numerous departments and individuals. Some companies have elaborate designs for their fax sheets. The fax covering sheet usually conveys the following:

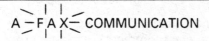

A – F A X – COMMUNICATION

from CLOTHSNIP CORPORATION
specialists in short trousers
Perseverance Works, Legge Street, Bradford BD99 9OK
Tel: .... Fax: ....

To: (Company)   Date:

Attention: (Name/Dept)   No of pages inc
this one:

From: (Name/Dept)   Reference:

Subject:

Note: if fax is not clearly received please telephone
098-7654321

You, being a bluff, no-nonsense captain of industry, can dispense with frills and simply write on a sheet of your company notepaper: FAX/To/From/Date/No of pages.

As with all good things, don't over-use the fax with, for example, repeated chasers or promotional offers to the same people. Reserve its speed and impact for situations where it can really move your business on a notch. You can connect your fax to your computer system to send invoices, dispatch notes etc directly down the line to customers.

Follow-ups

You can send a chaser if you haven't had a reply to your first letter. A follow-up letter may also be sent as an after-sales quality check, or you may send a follow-up with information which wasn't available earlier. A follow-up system is, of course, part and parcel of CREDIT CONTROL correspondence. See also REMINDER letters, you can also follow up by phone.

A follow-up when you haven't had a reply; send by fax

Dear —   [Date]

I have had no reply to my letter to you of...

May I remind you that we are waiting for the return of the signed agency contract? We cannot proceed with the dispatch of stock meanwhile.

Please send us your immediate reply.

A follow-up letter used as a feature of after-sales service.

Note the sting for the maintenance contract.

Dear Customer   [Date]

It is now a month since we installed your PIRANA office shredder.

We trust your PIRANA is giving trouble-free performance, devouring old documents and printouts and converting them into tasteful sacks of packing material, hamster bedding etc. He's very reliable and very voracious, is our shredder!

Thank you for becoming another PIRANA customer. This letter is part of our follow-up service to ensure your satisfaction. Our local rep, John Teeth, will call on you in the next few days to adjust the PIRANA now it is run in. He will also bring for your consideration our very moderate maintenance contract. Free service calls for three years! We would advise it – it's just a form of insurance, after all. Thanks again for choosing a Pirana!

Follow-up after phone call to send literature or samples and set up sales meeting

Dear friend   [Date]

Here is the information you asked for on the HEDGEHOG cosmetics range.

I'm sending the fabulous New Year colour range of samples plus a mini counter display pack. Compact but colourful. It can sit right next to your cash point.

There, the temptation to take a HEDGEHOG can be too much even for strong men! We've seen it in our market research and other retailers are confirming that all classes of consumer enjoy this product.

The enclosed literature covers the full range of stock and gives you up-to-the-minute prices. We have some special deals going for New Outlets, and I'd like to call by for 15 minutes in the next few days to tell you of our extra discounts and perhaps take your first trial order.

I'll telephone you to fix a convenient time. Thanks for having faith in HEDGEHOG!

With best wishes.

Yours sincerely

Edward Jogger
Sales Development Executive

Follow-up letter to close order, following inconclusive meeting

Dear Igor   [Date]

Your order

It was a pleasure meeting you on Tuesday.

I am writing to confirm that we would price the order
you were considering for...at £..., allowing, as you
observe, a special discount. I can also say that I have
prepared the way in our order processing and packing
departments so your order will go through smoothly
and promptly. I hope to receive your confirmation by
return so that we can go ahead with supplying you on
the terms agreed. Our fax number is....

Many thanks, and with best wishes.

Yours sincerely

Boris Smith
Sales Manager

Follow-up after meeting prospect at trade show

Dear Miss Leaper   [Date]

Many thanks for leaving your card at our stand at the
Soft Animals Trade Fair last week. It was a pleasure to
have your visit and I am only sorry that the pressure of
these events left us unable to ascertain your needs on
the spot.

I am enclosing our current literature – note the exciting
new Marsoopial product range! – and have asked Barry
Pouch, our soft animals specialist, to visit you in the
next few days. We remain at your disposal and look
forward to working with you.

Yours sincerely

Foreign correspondence

Don't expect your overseas correspondents to have a perfect knowledge of colloquial English. They usually speak and write it pretty well
anyway, and your own Japanese and Arabic probably aren't all that
hot. Write briefly, simply and unambiguously. Remember it's the
figures of speech that fox - sorry, puzzle people.

If you can muster any Western European languages, use them by
all means, especially French. Unless your French is ridiculous and
execrable, make the attempt. The French appreciate Francophiles,
and it's worth taxing your linguistic capabilities if the result is a
business lunch in Paris, though that sounds like cupboard love rather
than Francophilia. Letters from Italy and Spain quite often come in
their respective languages, not that Italians or Spaniards care particularly what language is used. But if you can write a letter they can
understand, you have a better chance of a reply. Translation agencies
abound, of course - at a price.

Take care, when writing abroad, to get the address right. German
letterheads in particular have a habit of running the phone number
straight after the address. More than once have I found, when idly
flicking through the letters to be posted, that the unfortunate typist
has put (for example):

R Schrecken GmbH
1000 Berlin
Zigeunerallee 27
Fernruf 30 49 18 20

- presumably so that the postman could ring up from a kiosk if he
couldn't find the address.

Above all, in letters sent overseas, be courteous. Other nations
often have high standards in such matters. It is not only good manners; cultivate some warmth in your letters and you will have the
sense of human contact across the continents. Send your best wishes
and your recollection of a pleasant visit there - or send, perhaps, an
invitation to visit you and meet your colleagues and family.

Goodwill

Goodwill is what you have a hard job getting cash for when you sell
your business. Goodwill is the momentum of a business. Goodwill is
the likelihood that customers will come back for more. Goodwill

even generates new customers, although not as well as marketing does.

Goodwill itself is generated out of the quality of a business. The quality is partly in the product, and partly in the service, or in the relationships between the company and the world outside. Accordingly, each day, your letters invisibly augment or diminish the company's goodwill.

It doesn't make much difference, you may say. In the ordinary way it doesn't. But try writing rude or illiterate letters, or not writing at all. You would notice the difference after a little while.

Headhunting, brain picking and information exchanges

Headhunting is customarily done by specialised agencies. It means contacting an individual in a company to offer him another job, either because he is personally known or because he commands wanted skills. Such individuals are usually at senior level and not necessarily on the lookout for a change, so there is a strong element of luring in the operation. Since the matter is delicate – sometimes a competitor wants to rustle a key man – the first approach is typically by telephone and the negotiation may remain verbal until agreement, or disagreement, is reached. You would write your proposals or offer to the target's home address.

You may not want to recruit your competitors but you may well want to discuss common problems with them, and they with you. Conferences provide a forum for just this, as well as for a night or two on the town for the jaded executive. You can always set up a meeting, on the following lines:

Dear Peter   [Date]

We are having a lot of problems at the moment with our new Wurst 3000 bagging system. I know you bought one of these recently – I wonder if we could put our heads together. I have one or two positive views on the subject; at worst we can present a concerted front to the supplier. I would be happy to stand you a lunch, perhaps next week some time.

Or if you feel sociable (or generous), you could set up a sort of luncheon club or meeting place for people in the same business.

Dear Peter   [Date]

I have been talking to one or two friends in the bagging systems business and there seems to be a shared interest in meeting from time to time to discuss common problems and brush up our ideas. Quite apart from having a good meal and a natter.

To start the ball rolling I will host a lunch for a very informal get-together. So far we have Roger Smith of Metro Bagging Corp who will come, Tony Fuller of Fuller Containers, and Oliver Twistle whom, of course, you know. The date in view is Friday 13 May, at the Smart Snail, where we will take a private room from around 12.30. Oliver has volunteered to give us his thoughts on 'Has bagging technology lost its way?' to stimulate some discussion.

I very much hope you can join us.

Import, see *Export/Import*

Insurance

Insurance matters may be complex in themselves, but should not normally need complex correspondence. If you have things organised for your convenience, all your insurances are handled by an agent who does practically everything for you. When you have an insurance claim you ring your agent who sends you a claim form. You send this off with a covering letter saying, 'Dear Sir, I enclose my completed claim form in respect of...', remarking on any points you want to draw attention to.

There is one very useful insurance letter, namely the 'please keep us covered' letter. If you have taken over new premises, leased a new machine, bought a new car or simply set off on holiday in Europe and forgotten to ask for a green card, write to your brokers as follows:

Dear Sirs   [Date]

Commercial combined policy [or Motor policy etc]

As from 9.00 am 1 April 1994 we shall be occupying an additional 1,000 sq ft of rented storage space at Peabody Mall/be responsible for insurance on a leased Pretzel photocopier and collator system value £10,000/be taking delivery of a Ferrari regd no L15 SOM value £85,000 for the sales fleet/be leaving for four weeks' holiday in France, Switzerland, Italy and Monaco in the Ferrari.

Please keep us covered and forward the necessary endorsements to our policy.

With thanks.

Yours faithfully

If, of course, you have a good relationship with your agent you don't even need to write, you just phone him from Dover.

Invitations

See also ACCEPTANCES and REFUSALS. If you are sending invitations you will know whether the function is formal or informal. Formal invitations are, of course, sent for formal functions, ie functions at which formal dress is worn. Formal invitations are written in the third person and are usually printed on cards. Printers know what to say. However, nowadays formal invitations are also sent for informal functions, so if the function is really formal you have to indicate this by putting *Black Tie* on the lower left corner of the invitation. It's unusual these days to see *White Tie* (ie evening dress) or if you have a waggish sense of humour you could put *Pink Tie* and see what the gentlemen turn up in. Or the ladies.

A formal invitation (for a formal function)

The Directors of Blackwitch Lingerie Ltd
request the pleasure of the company of
Mr J. F. Hammon-Stitch and companion
at a Fashion Show
followed by a Reception
on Thursday, 16 December 1993 at 5.00 pm
at The Grommets

RSVP
Fatima Sopcourse
Blackwitch Lingerie
The Grommets
Black Tie   Burnley

A formal invitation to an informal function

The Chairman and Directors of Purlop Corporation
request the pleasure of your company
at the Corporation's 21st Birthday Party
on Friday, 5 November at 6.00 pm

RSVP
Purlop Corporation
Purlop Hall
Buffet   Purlop

If you are sending informal invitations, anything goes. You can have funny cards printed. Or you can simply write to your friends as follows:

Dear Algy

We are having some informal drinks in the boardroom on Friday, 7 September at 6.00 pm to celebrate very quietly the publication of the 100th video in our History of Torture series. We do hope you and Dulcie will be able to join us.

Yours sincerely

Late payment see *Deferred payment*

Litigious letters

Legal letters strictly speaking are written by lawyers, to lawyers, and for lawyers. We have in this book certain instances where you have to write a business letter with the threat or the possibility of legal action arising from the issue at stake. In such cases you are advised to head your letter 'Without prejudice', so that the letter does not represent a final or unqualified statement on your part, rather as in the same way, when you are buying a house, you head the letter 'Subject to contract' so your letter does not represent an irrevocable offer or acceptance of an offer.

Every now and then we find ourselves more or less accidentally in correspondence with litigious persons – people who are ready to sue, or at least who threaten to sue, at the drop of a hat if they feel they have been slighted or the letter of agreement not observed.

You may also receive letters which are entirely correct, and you have a choice between doing the right thing or being sued. If your correspondent is wrong, there are various polite ways of dealing with the situation.

You receive the following letter:

Dear Sir

Without prejudice

We recently purchased from you the substantial quantity of 10 25-litre drums of Gungex Industrial Floor Sealing Compound. See your invoice no..., date..., value £...

The compound was put down in our workshop on 26–27 March. The intention was for the new floor to harden off over the Easter break.

However, it is now 10 April, and the floor is still in a tacky state. In fact it comes up on the men's boots like treacle and the workshop is to all intents and purposes unusable. Nothing can be put on the floor and a tool dropped on it becomes coated in bituminous compound.

May I hereby request your immediate attention to this matter, and your rectification of it. I point out that the material you supplied is obviously failing in its function as a floor, and we should be reimbursed for that outlay. Even more serious, we must consider our loss of time and loss of output through the failure in performance of this floor, and must indicate that we will be seeking compensation at a moderate but realistic level.

I expect to hear from you by return, as we view this matter with the utmost gravity.

Yours faithfully

What do you reply? Presumably you go and look at the floor. Your foreman takes one look, sticks his finger in it, and cries, 'Where's the hardener?'

'What hardener?', says the customer. You indicate cautiously that a hardening agent has to be mixed with the compound when it is laid, otherwise it stays like treacle. So it all depends on the hardener. If this order was the one that went out in a hurry towards the end of March to make the early sales close that month, and the hardener got forgotten, you're in trouble.

You write as follows:

Dear —   [Date]

Without prejudice

Your order for Gungex Floor Compound

Following your letter of...and our visit to your premises, we accept responsibility for the state of the floor, as we have found that the necessary hardening agent was omitted from the consignment.

We would like to express our great regret for the inconvenience you have suffered. We offer to undertake the following measures of reparation.

With immediate effect we are sending in a team to

relay the floor. This will be completed before the weekend and the floor will be usable Monday morning.

Regarding your possible claim for compensation we would like to discuss this matter with you at an early meeting. We would make two observations which we feel mitigate your claim. One, that you presumably have insurance cover for loss of profits from accidental causes. Two, that according to our records you purchased a quantity of Gungex Compound two years ago and apparently laid it successfully, with the implication that your staff should, with common sense and moderate memories, have recalled that a hardener is required to lay this floor.

From this point the amount of compensation, if any, is a matter for negotiation. But what if, when your foreman was poking the treacly compound, he had found some tins of hardener under a bench? You had delivered the hardener after all! Then you might write as follows:

Dear —   [Date]

Without prejudice

Your workshop floor

Following your letter of...and our visit to your premises, we have to report finding ten tins of hardener unopened under a bench in the workshop. The hardener is, of course, an essential ingredient of the floor, and the tacky state of the compound as we found it suggests that it was laid without hardener.

In these circumstances we cannot accept responsibility for the state of the floor, nor entertain your claim for compensation for lost time and work.

However, as a gesture of goodwill I am happy to put a couple of our men at your disposal for a day to help with putting down the hardener. Perhaps you would let me know if this would be helpful.

And so litigation is averted...but not always. There comes a point when, if a legitimate claim is resisted, you must put the papers in the hands of a solicitor. Perhaps his letters will then do the trick.

Lost letters

Occasionally letters get lost in the post. It doesn't happen often, but you can be sure it will happen on the only occasion the photocopy was thrown away or vital instructions have to reach the bank on Monday morning. When you find out that the letter never arrived you are usually speaking to the people on the phone, or reading their letter which would have been different if they had got yours. If events have not superseded it, you can send a photocopy of the letter, assuming you kept a copy, with a compliments slip.

Eventually your original letter is sent back to you from somewhere like Bangkok, having been opened to get at the sender's address and doubtless read with amazement at the strange letters other people write.

Love letters

Perhaps you still keep a bundle of love letters from your youth, preferably tied with a ribbon and definitely not from your spouse, in the bottom of the wardrobe, or behind a brick in the shed. You know better, of course, than to reread them, sensing the pathetic disillusion that might ensue.

In business, love letters have to be in code. They are quite rare, and quite an art form. They are also difficult to compose, so that it takes you all morning to devise a memo to Mrs Sperrold in marketing asking her to re-count the catalogue stock but which really means will she meet you in the snug bar of the Knackered Bull. By which time she has already gone out to lunch with her girlfriends.

Nor is it always a good idea to try to recapture moments of careless glory. Your first reaction, when you find you have to attend a conference in Strasbourg, is to write as follows:

Mademoiselle H Tressouple
...

My dear Hélène
I shall be in Strasbourg from 17 to 20 October to attend

the Sales Software Conference, and wonder if we could have dinner one evening to review some of our European marketing problems. I still think of last year's conference as a most valuable marketing experience.

But you either get no reply or you get this:

Dear Mr Ponsonby

Thank you for your letter. I regret that I am not participating to the conference this year.

Yours

Mme H Marchand

Don't despair! Whatever sex you are. Forget about sending sly messages. Wear your heart on your sleeve and send a note of sincere appreciation.

Dear Barbara [or Dear Walter]

Just a note to say how much I enjoyed meeting you last week and hearing what you had to say. I hope there will be another opportunity to talk before too long. Do let me know if business brings you in this direction and perhaps we could have lunch.

If you do go in for coded messages remember that too much mysterious activity will brand you as an eccentric or an industrial mole, which is much more embarrassing.

Mail order see Circulars and Direct mail

Memoranda

Some companies have memos flashing round their departments like the Rocky Mountains have lightning flickering round Twin Peaks. The BBC is said to be better at generating memos than programmes. Memos are like internal letters. People who are not on speaking terms can send each other frosty, point-scoring memos.

The memorandum (plural: memoranda; memo for short) is an old-fashioned and useful thing. It means: something to be remembered. If you have a good idea for a new product, so the idea doesn't get lost set it down in a memorandum from yourself to the new projects file (with a copy to your boss).

Moratorium see *Deferred payment*

No thank you letters

When you can't, or don't want to, attend a function for which you have had a formal invitation, you reply as follows:

> Mr J Q Kanobe thanks the Directors of Pencil Corporation for their kind invitation, but regrets he is unable to attend.

If you are declining an informal invitation, you could write like this:

> Dear Martin
>
> Many thanks for your kind invitation for 20 January. I am afraid I am already committed for that day, and won't be able to come.

Or in a particularly friendly vein:

> Dear Martin
>
> So kind of you to ask me for the 20th. I am furious that I have to be away that day and can't make it. But let's meet anyway, perhaps early next month.

Declining an offer of employment

Dear Mr — [Date]

Thank you very much for your letter of...offering me the position of...

However, I have thought the matter over carefully since our meeting and have decided not to accept the post after all, for personal as well as career reasons.

I very much appreciate your offer, and am sorry if I have caused you any inconvenience.

Declining an offer of services

Dear Mr Repton [Date]

Thank you for your recent visit and your offer of a freelance repping service.

Your proposal was interesting but I am afraid that we cannot justify investing in such a service at present. Thank you for coming to see me.

The ultimate no thank you letter

For use when you want to indicate polite exasperation and polite finality.

Dear — [Date]

No thank you.

Yours sincerely

See also REFUSALS and REJECTIONS

Offers

You can offer employment, assistance, money, services. Remember that a written offer is, as the lawyers say, binding. That is why you should head certain kinds of offer 'Subject to contract', so that the offer is not prematurely and unconditionally enforceable, such cases occurring particularly when you are purchasing property or other assets.

For offers of employment, see EMPLOYMENT.

For a letter offering to take over a lease, see PREMISES.

Making an offer for an asset

Dear —   [Date]

Offer for your Winkelberg 400 offset printing machine

Following our earlier discussions and our inspection of this machine we would like to make the following offer to purchase it.

We have in mind that the machine is now five years old and the estimated maintenance charge over the next five years is likely to average £...pa. We also bear in mind that we will be undertaking removal and transportation. We might add that we observe some oil seepage and roller wear on the machine.

Our offer is accordingly £...We propose paying one half of this sum on your acceptance of our offer, and one half one month after successful installation and running of the machine.

This offer lapses one month from the date of this letter. We look forward to hearing from you meanwhile.

Offering services

This is really a kind of sales letter.

Dear Mr —   [Date]

Market research report service

Following our telephone call to you today, I am herewith setting out our offer to provide your firm with a tailor-made market research report system geared to your particular interests.

For a set subscription per annum we provide an initial annual report plus three quarterly updates on your chosen marketplace. For the purposes of this proposal, you suggested one report on the structure of the pick-up truck and four-wheel drive market excluding family vehicles.

We offer an initial report of approximately 100 pages covering manufacturers, current models, history of discontinued models, market shares and buyer segment analysis. Per quarter we report on changing market shares, new models, discernible trends and one special feature per quarter, eg the impact of the power take-off (PTO) option on the pick-up market.

The subscription for this service is currently on special offer and we would supply the annual report plus three updates for the annual sum of £...This subscription buys our basic private circulation report. We are, of course, able to furnish additional research features at your behest, the additional charge being negotiable.

We look forward to your acceptance of this market information offer.

Orders

If you don't have printed order stationery or if you are not locked into a computer-based purchasing system, you can use your company letterhead to order, and you don't need to write a letter about it either. Letters used to be written on the lines: 'We beg the favour of placing with your goodselves an ORDER for 1 doz. doz. (one gross) handkerchieves, gents', white linen, large size, plain edging. Looking forward to an early delivery and the favour of your best terms, we remain, Your respectful servants.'

Such a letter would doubtless do the trick and would probably get framed as well by your amazed suppliers. Alternatively you may care to commend your order to the post (or to the fax) in the following manner. Order numbers should be used for subsequent reference, including allocation of payments received.

Zonal Corporation Ltd
Corporation St
Old Milton Keynes
Bucks MK87 1AA

Order no S7/007   Order date:

Please supply:

1 female zoning system model ZC84 with castors and dust cover.

At our usual trade terms.

Please deliver to address below.

(Signed) Marketing Manager
City Research Co
Research House
Research Street
Research City

Order processing

Order processing is another systematic activity which is best done with pre-printed forms allocating job numbers, stock locations, prices etc. If a customer acknowledgement is required this can also be done by a pre-printed postcard carrying a range of responses with boxes for the appropriate one to be ticked. See ACKNOWLEDGE-MENTS.

From time to time, or in a business involving one-off and complex orders, the order processing department needs to write to the customer. The information to be imparted is: acknowledge order; discuss special needs; quote delivery and price.

Dear Customer   [Date]

Thank you for your order, date...for...This item is not in

stock at present; we expect to order a batch in ten days' time.

We note you ask for the fur-trim option. This was discontinued last year but we will supply the improved velour model unless you instruct us otherwise.

We expect therefore to ship this order by approximately 10 September.

The price including the velour option and the castors you specify will be £5,975.00.

Yours sincerely

Margaret Devereux
Order Department

The previous order raises the question whether an item with velour option and castors should be shipped on credit if it is adding £5,975.00 to your risky debtors. Part of the function of order processing, therefore, is to distinguish between credit account customers and pro-forma or pre-pay customers. The latter receive a similar but different letter (or a standard form).

Dear Customer   [Date]

PRO-FORMA INVOICE

Thank you for your order, date...for...Your order can be delivered on approximately 10 September at a price of £...

We regret that we cannot supply this order on credit terms, and accordingly request your prepayment. Our pro-forma invoice is enclosed and your order will be ready for shipment when we receive your remittance.

We thank you for your order.

Yours sincerely

Deirdre Rush
Order Processing

Premises

If you move offices you may find that you can take over an existing lease from the previous occupants at a historic rent. In which case the outgoing company may 'sell' you the lease for a premium, this being a sum negotiated somewhere below the difference between the value of the unexpired old rental period and the cost of taking a new lease at the market rate. Conversely you can look for a premium from the incoming company when you are vacating offices with a cheap rental.

For the most part correspondence over leases – particularly new ones – will be handled by your solicitor. But if you want to take over an unexpired lease you may need to write as follows. The letter doesn't specifically make an offer but it is intended to convey that, subject to negotiating a satisfactory offer, you will instruct your solicitor to go ahead. The letter also indicates that you have checked the measurements and that you are not interested in buying all the fixtures and fittings the outgoing party would like to pick up some cash for.

Letter expressing desire to take over lease on office space

Dear —   [Date]

Re: First floor office suite, Olympic House, Potherwick

Following my several visits to your property, together with my colleagues, I confirm my strong interest in acquiring from you your existing lease in regard to the above office suite.

I have, of course, had a sight of the lease but I would be grateful to receive a copy of it from your solicitors, Plimsoll, Line & Co.

I have also measured the offices and in fact I calculate that the net floor area is 1,398 sq ft with, in addition, the WC and kitchenette. On the basis of the net floor area, the rent calculates at £...per sq ft.

I would need to redecorate the offices completely and

would also recarpet, though I would like to purchase from you the existing electric wall heaters.

Perhaps we could meet in the immediate future at some mutually convenient date to discuss the question of the premium.

Price increase

Price increases should be notified in various ways. The prime way is to establish a pattern of an annual catalogue (issued in October/November the previous year) carrying the new year's prices. This is for the benefit of customers at large. You may need to write letters notifying special customers – eg customers with standing orders or subscriptions – and to your agents, distributors and representatives.

To all representatives and agents

From: A Tobin, Marketing Director   [Date]

PRICE INCREASES

Please note the following price increases operative from 1 December:

Home cookery series: all titles by 15 per cent

Home knitting series:
Relative increases, see attached schedule (A)
Average increase 13.5 per cent

Home jam-making series:
Existing titles no change
Forthcoming titles plus 25 per cent on planned levels
Revised schedule (B) attached

These increases are to be explained as a response to increased production costs over the last year which in fact have squeezed our margins by 20 per cent so these price increases fall a little short of making up that margin. We have been as aggressive as we feel is possible in present market conditions. We are considering a further overall increase of 10 per cent at mid-year but will consult with you again before any further change.

You need at times to write to a customer who thinks he can still buy a thingummy or a copy of his grandmother's fairytales from you for sixpence. Occasionally you get stamps or postal orders or cheques for 75p, the balance being 'to cover the postage'. You write as gently as you can.

Dear Mr Thumble   [Date]

Thank you very much for your kind order for...and your remittance as well.

Unfortunately time has moved on so fast, and inflation too, that the price of this item is now £19.95.

I hesitate to send it as you were expecting to pay so much less. Perhaps you could let me know if you do want it at the increased price. I am sorry that prices have risen so, but look forward meanwhile to hearing whether you want us to send your order or not.

If yes, could you send a new cheque for £19.95?

Thank you so much.

Yours sincerely

Dora Posit
Order Processing

Explaining a price increase to a private (non-trade) customer

---

Dear Revd Golightly   [Date]

We appreciate your concern over the price increases in our...product line.

In fact this is the first increase for a considerable period, and we have resisted considerable pressures in the interest of price stability. But materials and subcontract labour costs have gone up by over...per cent over the last year. Our own overheads including wages, rents, fuel costs, have all increased. None of these factors is within our control. We must now increase our prices, otherwise we face unprofitability and the decline of our business.

I am sure you appreciate these hard facts. I thank you for taking the trouble to communicate with us and hope we can improve our standards of service to you as a valued customer.

Notifying price increase to a trade customer

No need to explain. In some businesses, it is customary to announce price increases via the trade press.

To our customers   [Date]

Notice of price increase

There will be an across-the-board price increase of 5 per cent applied to our...product line with effect from 1 March 19...

Progress reports

See also REPORTS. Progress reports should be set out in checklist form or with a series of headings. The report may well be a separate document, sent with a brief covering letter. Otherwise the letter-type formalities can be kept to a minimum, as follows:

Dear —   [Date]

New Craft Centre – monthly progress report for February 19...

Herewith my progress report on the start-up of the new centre for the month just ended.

1. Building work. The builders are now completing plastering and plumbing in the extension. The extra space is expected to be habitable by 31 March.

2. Craft centre display area. This is now fully prepared and 340 visitors were received in February against 203 in January. Some improvements remain to be made to the display itself.

3. Craft activity. A potter was recruited last month so we now have both a potter and a weaver at work. We have received an approach from a local fabric printer which is being considered.

4. Commercial report. Net sales invoiced in February rose to £2,700 (January £2,100), of which £800 was taken at the till and the balance shipped to Group Sales at transfer price.

5. Outlook. Some way to go before we can see real build-up in sales. Next month's priorities: conclude building work; finalise local publicity plans.

6. Documents attached: (a) month's profit and loss account; (b) updated cash flow statement and forecast.

Best wishes.

Yours sincerely

F Pownall
Craft Centre Manager

Proposals

The proposal is one of the key communications in business life: the written instrument of change. When you write a proposal you formulate an idea, justify the idea, show how it may be put into practice, and forecast the outcome. A proposal may also be an offer if, for example, you send a proposal to buy something. But for the most part a proposal is a plan of action; when you want something doing, you invite proposals.

Suppose you have under-used resources in a particular department; there might be the following exchange of letters between two senior managers or between the company and an outside consultant.

Dear Anita   [Date]

The company's market data department

Following changes in the company's organisation we find we are not making proper use of the former market data department, consisting of two researchers and a rather extensive database of ongoing market information.

We are reluctant to close the department and disperse the data and know-how which represent a considerable investment over the years. Could you analyse the activities and expertise of the department, review possible applications and developments, and let me have your proposals?

Dear Jane   [Date]

Market data dept – a proposal for its redevelopment

We have examined this department as instructed and submit herewith our detailed proposal for your consideration (see enclosure).

We may summarise our findings as follows:

1. We agree that the department represents a valuable resource which should not be dispersed.

2. We propose that the department be developed into a specialised publishing operation producing and selling market reports.

3. This development would entail the recruitment of two persons and an investment over two years of £...

4. The new operation is expected to generate:
after two years: sales £...; profit contribution £...
after five years: sales £...; profit contribution £...

5. In conclusion, this proposal shows that a resource

at present lying fallow may, with some input of
cash and management attention, be turned into a
productive unit.

We shall be glad to discuss our conclusions in detail
and suggest a meeting next week at which we may
present our proposals to your management review
group.

Good proposals, it might be concluded, are a young person's way to
the top, and not just in marriage. If you want to set up something
new, or bring about change, send your boss a proposal. What she or
he does about it is another matter.

We give here a checklist for the structure of a business proposal –
in summarised form.

BUSINESS PROPOSAL CHECKLIST   [Date]

1. Management summary
   - The recommendations
   - Key financial information
   - Key operating features

2. Background information
   - Historical perspective
   - Rationale for the proposal

3. Information about the proposal
   - Concept, description, specification
   - Development process and cost
   - Timetable

4. Marketing information
   - Market size and structure
   - Key sectors/targets
   - Competition
   - Marketing strategy
   - Promotional plans

5. Financial information
   - Sales and profit forecast
   - Cash flow analysis
   - Investment requirement

6. Risks and problems

7. Appendices: detailed plans, schedules

Quotations

A quotation is an offer to sell goods or supply services for a stated price, as distinct from an estimate, which can be amended as the work proceeds.

An overseas bookseller asks you to quote for the supply of 100 sets of your *Pacific Basin Encyclopaedia*. Quotations should indicate that prices are firm until a given date. Send by fax if possible.

Dear Sheila   [Date]

Quotation for 100 sets, Pacific Basin Encyclopaedia
We thank you for your enquiry of...and quote as follows:

Pacific Basin Encyclopaedia. 8,250 pages including colour and black and white illustrations, bound in 16 vols. Page size 9 x 6 in. Library binding. List price £320 per set.

We can quote you at an exceptional discount of 60 per cent off list price, ie at £128 per set or £12,800 for the consignment. Surface shipment would be charged at £450.

Payment would be by bank transfer or cheque at 90 days from date of invoice.

We stress, however, that this offer, because of the exceptional discount and limited stocks remaining, is open for 28 days only from the date of this letter. Please fax your acceptance and we look forward to hearing from you.

The offer entailed in a quotation you receive may not suit you. If you write back haggling or varying the terms you are in effect making a counter-offer.

Dear Sirs [Date]

Your quotation ref...for 100 window frames

Thank you for your letter and price for supplying the above. We would like to deal with you because of our past relationship and the quality of your work. May we, however, press you on your price. We feel you are not as competitive as when we bought from you last year.

We would be looking for either 5 per cent extra discount or 120 days' credit from your date of invoice.

If you can confirm your agreement to one of these courses we will let you have our order by return.

Recruitment

The recruitment process starts either with you placing an advertisement or contacting a recruitment agency. Define the job specification for the post in question and base your advertisement or your agency briefing on that. See also EMPLOYMENT, offers of.

Acknowledging an application

Dear Mr/Mrs/Miss/Ms — [Date]

This is to acknowledge with thanks your application for the position of...

I am considering the applications received and will be in touch with you again shortly.

Inviting a candidate to interview

Dear Mr/Mrs/Miss/Ms — [Date]

Further to your application for the position of...,I should be glad if you would come for an interview.

> Could you please ring my office to arrange a convenient time. We will reimburse your travel expenses.
>
> I look forward to meeting you.

Redundancy

Write no redundancy letters without being sure of the legal provisions prevailing at the time. We give a guide to the way you might phrase the letters, but check the provisions as the law changes from time to time. Bear in mind also that the financial compensation for redundancy required by law is only a minimum. In some circumstances you may want to be, or perhaps should be, more generous.

When you have a number of people to write to about impending redundancy, write to them individually. As far as possible the letter should follow up a meeting where the matter is disclosed in a personal and compassionate way. And do not write to people in their pay packets – not that you would. Treat them with dignity. If there is a recognised trade union in the company, there are requirements for consultation before any redundancies are declared. Small-scale redundancies are often made on the 'last in, first out' basis – recent employees have the least security. Alternatively volunteers are called for, with more generous compensation as an incentive.

Redundancies may arise as a result of reorganisation in a company, when certain jobs or departments cease to exist. The pretext of reorganisation, or rather the manipulation of responsibilities and new labelling for jobs, is sometimes used to bring about the redundancy of a problem manager.

Redundancy always was a sensitive issue. Now that redundancy is seen as a tributary of the great modern river of unemployment, it is a social as well as a business problem for the company.

A letter to each of a number of employees in a department to say that there will have to be redundancies, and offering generous compensation for volunteers

> Dear —   [Date]
>
> It is no secret that the company has been going

through a hard time this year. Sales have fallen, costs as ever have increased, and we have not been making the profit necessary to keep the business healthy.

The company now has to make savings wherever possible. I have the unpleasant responsibility of reducing our labour costs by making a number of redundancies. In all, we must cut ten jobs from this department by the end of the year.

To avoid imposing unnecessary hardship on any of you, we have decided to try to achieve the necessary reduction in jobs by voluntary redundancies. Accordingly we are offering liberal financial compensation, well over the statutory minimum. We are offering generous terms even for short-service staff, whose entitlement under the law is not very much.

This could be an opportunity for those of you who may have thought of making a break or setting up on your own, but always lacked that extra bit of finance.

We are sorry to have to make this announcement, especially as so many of you have given so many years' service to the company. But at this moment of economic crisis, we have little choice. I hope the necessary redundancies can be achieved by voluntary leavers. Will those interested please come and see me to discuss redundancy terms in confidence.

A letter to an employee announcing the closure of a department and stating redundancy terms

Remember to take expert advice on the legal provisions in force when you write.

Dear —   [Date]

I am sorry to tell you that, following the takeover of this company, the Cutting Department is to be closed. We are unable to find alternative work for you and must therefore terminate your employment, with one month's notice, on grounds of redundancy.

The minimum compensation required by law is one week's pay for every year or part year of service, assuming a minimum of two years' service. You have been with us for... years, and your current gross wage is £...pw. This makes the minimum for you... x £...=£...

We would like to make more generous compensation than the legal minimum, and propose making a payment to you of £...This sum will be tax free and will be paid to you, in addition to your final pay packet, on the day your employment ceases, ie on 31 May.

May I thank you for your loyal service to this company and express my regret that for reasons beyond our control we must end your employment in this way.

References

If you are considering a person for a job, you may want to take up their references. The simplest way to do this is by phone. That way you get a more honest verdict on the candidate because it doesn't have to be put in writing. The previous employer may be more likely to speak to you openly after receipt of an introductory letter from you to establish your bona fides.

When you write to a sizeable organisation, it is helpful if you say when the applicant worked for them so the file can be tracked down quickly. It is also usual to enclose a stamped addressed envelope. If you want a written reference you write to the referee as follows:

Dear Mr Parrot   [Date]

We are considering Miss Frankie Ferlmutter for the post of Product Manager, Soft Toy Division. This position entails marketing and budgetary responsibility and control of a small department of staff.

She has given us your name as a reference and I would be most grateful for your opinion, in the strictest confidence, on her suitability for the post. I understand she was employed by you from 19.. to June 19...

The opinion you get, of course, depends whether the reference comes from a former employer or from a 'character reference' such as very old ladies, local vicars and school teachers who can't remember which one you were.

When it is your turn to write a reference the same applies. If you feel strongly about the candidate you can ring up the dazed interviewer and cry, 'Don't on any account employ this person!'

Or you can send the usual character reference, which runs approximately as follows:

Dear Sir   [Date]

In response to your letter of 7 July I am very happy to supply a reference for Miss Peabody.

I have known Esther Peabody for 5/10/25 years and have always found her a most pleasant and trustworthy person. I am sure she would be an excellent choice.

Yours faithfully

There is a sort of convention that you don't do the dirty on a person in a reference so that references frequently read with a predictable sameness about fundamentally decent, exceptionally reliable, personally pleasant etc. We well know that such letters are bland lies, either because you are indifferent to the matter and can't be bothered to recall what the person was really like, or because it would be churlish to tell the truth and spoil the candidate's chances. There are ways, as we shall see, of encoding an unfavourable opinion.

The following are favourable references of one sort of another. First, a reference for a person of undoubted competence (who presumably once worked for you).

I am happy to recommend Mr...In his years with us he showed himself to be a reliable and hard working person with a capacity for original ideas as well as close attention to detail. He was good at organising his work and got on well with people around him.

A reference for someone you like who may or may not be any good at their job

> I can wholeheartedly recommend Miss...She has a friendly and outgoing personality and is capable of flashes of brilliance in her work. She is a very willing person and an asset in the office.

A dull but solid reference

> In answer to your enquiry, Mr...can be depended on to produce accurate work and, in matters of confidentiality or finance, is a man of quiet integrity.

Then there are references where you feel you should at least pull the curtain a little to one side and give the prospective employer a hint of your real opinion.

A reference when you don't want to damn the person's chances altogether but feel you should say: beware! to the new employer.

> You asked us for a reference.
>
> Mr...worked for us for five years as a sales assistant. He was always punctual and polite.

Or, in more explicit terms.

> Mr...was our sales manager for a short period in 1993. He has an engaging and plausible personality and our expectations went up before sales went down.

Refusals

See also NO THANK YOU letters

A refusal is firm but polite. You are refusing something somebody wants; as ever you have a choice in the way you do it. If you don't care what the other person thinks or feels, you can be curt or you can refuse politely, even reluctantly in some cases.

A curt refusal

Dear Sir

Thank you for your offer. We do not require the service you propose.

A polite refusal

Dear Mr —

Many thanks for your marketing proposal.

We have read it with interest but feel, after serious consideration, that we do not wish to go ahead with the project for the time being.

With best wishes.

A reluctant refusal

Dear Larry

Thank you for your recent letter offering stock at reduced prices.

We should very much like to take advantage of this offer but unfortunately do not have the funds available at present.

Please bear us in mind should a future opportunity arise.

Refusing to see a rep or to receive a sales presentation

Dear Mr —

Thank you for your letter and phone call requesting an appointment to discuss your services.

We are fully committed to our existing suppliers at present and it would not be worthwhile looking at alternatives. [or: This is not an area in which we wish to commit funds at present and it would not be worthwhile arranging a meeting.]

Refusing credit to a customer

Dear Sir

Thank you for your order ref...

We regret we do not have enough information at present to grant our usual credit terms. [or: We regret that we can only supply individual (or overseas) customers on a pre-paid basis.]

We enclose our pro-forma invoice and have your order ready for shipment as soon as we receive your payment.

Rejections

It used to be the thing for aspiring writers to paper the loo with their rejection slips. Rejection slips are a kind of opposite of compliments slips. They usually say something like: The Editor thanks you for your submission but regrets he cannot make use of it.

Rejection is a rather severe expression; turning down or declining is less of a shock to the system. In business you do have to reject - usually unsuccessful applications, occasionally unwelcome accusations.

Rejecting a job application before shortlist or interview stage

> Dear —   [Date]
>
> Thank you for your application for the post of...
>
> Owing to the large number of applications we have received, we have been obliged to close the list and cannot therefore consider you for the position.

Rejecting an applicant after interview (or rather, telling him he has been unsuccessful)

> Dear —   [Date]
>
> I am sorry to say that we are unable to offer you the position of...which we recently discussed.
>
> Thank you for your interest in the job and for taking the trouble to come and see us.
>
> With best wishes.

Rejecting an allegation or claim. See also *Litigious letters.*

A rejection letter of a different kind.

> Dear Sir   [Date]
>
> Thank you for your letter of...claiming that our last shipment to you was wrongly invoiced and overcharged.
>
> We must disagree with your claim, as increases in price and carriage charges were faxed to you on 13 August. There seems to have been an error on your part in this matter.

Reminder letters

If you are waiting for a response you can send a very short letter plus a copy of the original.

Dear —   [Date]

We are waiting for a reply to our letter to you of..., and enclose a further copy.

We would appreciate your immediate attention to the matter.

You can also, or if there is still no reply, send the above or a variant of it by fax. You can also telephone to see what's going on.

Reports

Reports are, strictly speaking, a whole subject to themselves. A report is different from a letter in format and style. Reports are written with headings and lists and often in note form. A short report can perfectly well be contained in a letter; but if a report goes beyond, say, a page in length, it should be separated off as an independent document, and sent with a covering letter. See also PROGRESS REPORTS and PROPOSALS for checklist structures for reports and similar documents.

You may, however, have to write a letter presenting an informal report.

Dear Henry   [Date]

May I report informally on the state of affairs I found on my visit to the West Bromwich factory.

My first impression was of untidiness and neglect. The yard was littered with scrap and there were one or two broken windows.

Inside the level of activity seemed low with a number of machines standing idle. There were some men at work, but morale did not appear very good. I didn't see any goods leaving the building at all.

The manager confided to me that he thought their work was being run down deliberately and he expected to be closed down sooner or later.

My recommendations to you are:

(a) Don't place any further work with them;
(b) Seek written assurances from their group headquarters that the jobs we have with them will be despatched to time;
(c) Pull existing work out ASAP, in the absence of (b).

We are due to meet next week.

Yours sincerely

Representation

A letter appointing a freelance sales representative – could apply also to a repping service company

See also AGENTS AND DISTRIBUTORS

Dear Mr Galahad   [Date]

This is to confirm that we appoint you to undertake sales representation for this company on the following terms:

1. The territory to be covered is Northern England, namely Liverpool–Manchester–Sheffield and north to Carlisle–Newcastle.

2. The duration of the agreement is for one year firm and thereafter is subject to three months' notice on either side, subject also to termination at shorter notice in the event of a breach by either party.

3. You will have the exclusive right to represent our brands, but will not carry competitive brands.

4. You will sustain repeat business with existing customers and also seek new customers.

5. Your minimum sales targets are 20 per cent overall sales growth per annum; 100 new customers per annum; and a steady increase in major customers and their repeat business (customers spending £10,000+ pa).

6. Your commission will consist of 0.5 per cent on all existing sales arising in the territory, and 10 per cent of new orders. Commission will be paid monthly on cash received.

7. You will send us a weekly visits report and a monthly sales report (see outline format attached).

8. We will supply product information and promotional material for your regular use.

Please send us a reply indicating your acceptance of these terms and we may then consider the agreement to be in force.

Good luck!

Requests

Requests are mostly requests for information or assistance, and may be very simply expressed.

Request for technical information

Dear Sirs   [Date]

Grass King mower series

Could you please send prices and parts lists, as well as details of available technical information and maintenance manuals, for this series.

With thanks.

Yours faithfully

Request for rep's visit and demonstration

> Dear Sirs [Date]
>
> We are interested in evaluating your HYENA word processing system, and should be grateful if you would arrange for your representative to visit us, bringing a demonstration model.
>
> Yours faithfully

Request for assistance where there is no commercial incentive, eg with completing a questionnaire

Address to a named recipient for maximum attention. It may be valuable to support the application with a phone call.

> Dear Mr Hurry [Date]
>
> May I request a few moments of your assistance with an inter-firm survey we are conducting.
>
> The enclosed brief questionnaire seeks details of your experience with photocopiers over the last two years.
>
> It should only take you five minutes to complete and return to us – but it could eventually lead to developments in the products you use.
>
> I can assure you of anonymity, and thank you in advance for your co-operation, in the interest of improving the business services we all use.

Resignation

Resigning is a rather rare thing which people who credit themselves with a certain status do, for example, politicians. Most of us just hand in our notice. However, there are circumstances where you may decide to resign, over a question of principle or if you are badly treated or passed over. Likewise there are circumstances when you can ask for a person's resignation, as a way of firing him or her which allows a more dignified exit.

A letter of resignation on grounds of principle or because of a personal clash

There may be the question of financial compensation which is not mentioned in this letter.

Dear Harriet [Date]

I have decided to resign my responsibilities with the company with effect at the earliest possible moment.

As you know, recent differences of opinion have made my position very difficult and I would rather bow out than continue in an atmosphere of compromise or pretence.

In the circumstances it seems undesirable that I should work out a period of notice and perhaps we could agree on a convenient date of departure.

Handing in your notice in a routine way – probably because you have got another job

Normally you write to your boss in the first instance. In fact, you usually tell him before you confirm it in writing.

Dear P J [Date]

This is to give notice of my intention to leave the company with effect one month from the end of this week, ie at 28 April.

I have accepted a position with another company which represents a considerable career advance, and I am eager to take it.

I would like to thank you for the experience I have gained and the support I have enjoyed during my time here.

I will, of course, round off the work I have had in hand, and leave my colleagues well briefed on anything outstanding when the time comes for me to leave.

Sales letters

See also CIRCULARS, DIRECT MAIL and FOLLOW-UPS.

Sales letters to prospects can be written with the particular aim of creating a lead, that is, an opening for a meeting or a sales presentation.

A lead-creating letter to a trade prospect

Dear friend   [Date]

This letter is your voucher for a glass of wine. Or two if you play your cards right.

We saw you last year, looking round at all those other confusing shelving systems.

There's only one to take seriously. It has the remarkable Rotamek TM in/out stock-turn facility. It has stacking height to 6m. It practically self-erects, with no nuts 'n' bolts but a lever-locking device that tightens as loads increase.

Plus your favourite permutations of lengths, breadths, heights, widths. Plus some wild colours to brighten those dingy stores of yesteryear. In fact our catalogue with its arrays of order pick systems and fancy gloves and roll-away units is a Christmas mail-order feast brought to your desk. And we don't charge more than some people we could mention.

What happened to those glasses of wine? Oh yes...They'll be waiting for you. Stand 406 at the Stacking Systems Fair, 1–4 April, at the Barbecue Conference Centre.

Looking forward to seeing you. Cheers!

Shippers

It is often convenient to employ the services of a shipping and forwarding agent to despatch export consignments too bulky to be posted. The shipper will attend to the packing and documentation and, if necessary, the payment. Communicate by fax.

Letter instructing shipping and forwarding agent

Dear Sirs   [Date]

Please pack with adequate protection and despatch by air freight the following consignment:

Books, one set Minerals Yearbook 1976-1995.

20 vols, weight 18kg, invoice value £880 including £80 provision for carriage and handling, by air freight

Customer: Documentation Department
                  University of Riyadh
                  Saudi Arabia

We enclose four copies of our certified invoice and will deliver the consignment to your premises on...Please fax us with flight no and ETA [Estimated Time of Arrival] and air waybill no as soon as known so we can fax these onward to the customer for his customs clearance.

Imported goods also come via shipping and forwarding agents. You may need to accept a bill of exchange, presentable at a later date, or otherwise arrange payment through your bank, before the goods are released from the inbound shipping agent. You would write to them as follows:

Dear Sirs   [Date]

Shipment of 100 bunk beds
from Bunkex Co Bucharest
to Bedland, Northampton

This is to confirm that we have today instructed our bank, ...Bank plc of..., to arrange a transfer of US $6,000 in payment of Bunkex Co's invoice no 860017.

When you receive notification of completed payment,

kindly release the consignment and convey it to our warehouse at:

Unit 4
Milton Friedman Trading Estate
Northampton

With thanks.

Staff letters

A staff letter or bulletin – the precursor of a house magazine – can be a useful device for welding your workforce into one happy family. What you put in your staff letter is up to you. You can design it like the parish magazine. An inspirational word or two from the Chairman (ie God), encouraging people to do good and love their neighbour. Then a more businesslike address from the Vicar – or rather, the managing director, reminding us of our monthly targets. One or two parables about talents or the prodigal manager. Then a social section about new arrivals, funerals and the horticultural show. Finally a competition. And what about a lonely hearts section? There's your staff letter for you.

Status enquiries

A status enquiry checks the credit status of a new customer. You may check both the company's financial standing with the bank (see BANK REFERENCES, CREDIT REFERENCES), and its track record with other customers it does business with (see TRADE REFERENCES).

Strong letters

You often hear people say, 'Write them a strong letter!' What is a strong letter, and how do you write one? It seems to mean: tell them exactly how you feel. Usually you write a strong letter when you are angry about something and want amends to be made. See ANGRY letters.

Let us see how you can express strong feelings in calm language. You should avoid abuse. You can be critical and perhaps sarcastic.

Suppose you have a machine which has broken down; eventually the engineer comes, it breaks down again, you can't get the suppliers to send anybody...after a number of phone calls you are at your wits' end.

You write first to the sales manager.

Dear Mr Middling   [Date]

We have been waiting three days for your engineer to attend to our model...machine.

You may recall the profuse assurances of speedy service and impeccable attention you gave us when we were deciding to buy the machine. Neither your personal assurance nor your company's service seems to carry much weight at this moment.

I am extremely disappointed that we should be treated in this way and ask you to rectify matters without further delay. Could we perhaps hear from you by phone and have an engineer's visit as soon as you receive this letter?

If you still get no satisfaction, you write to the boss - the managing director or director responsible. You find out his or her name first.

Dear Mrs Topping   [Date]

I am sorry to have to bring the following matter to your attention.

We bought your model...machine on 28.2.19... A week last Wednesday on 23.7.19.. it stopped working. Your engineer called next day and it worked fitfully for a few hours until breaking down again. Since then we have not been able to secure a service call despite telephoning repeatedly. I also wrote to your sales manager, Mr..., four days ago, by fax and first class post, without response.

It appears from this dismal treatment of a customer not only that your organisation is incapable of providing adequate after-sales service but that you are also indifferent to the consequences, since no one has attempted to communicate with us in over a week. We are not impressed by opportunist sales efforts without responsible service back-up.

In this letter I will not dwell on the cost to us of this extended downtime, plus the cost of phone calls and the discourtesy factor, in the hope that you can quickly set matters to rights. Please repair our machine – and repair the reputation of your company at the same time.

Takeovers see *Acquisitions*

Tenders

A tender is an offer to supply goods or carry out work, usually in response to a public advertisement and often in conformity with detailed specifications and conditions. The customer invites tenders by a given date and awards the project to the one preferred. Projects put out to tender are often complex construction or industrial works, sometimes in the public domain. In theory companies submitting tenders do so in ignorance of the tenders submitted by their competitors. Tenders are also invited for smaller exercises; for example, a company liquidator or receiver in bankruptcy proceedings may invite sealed bids for business stocks or other assets for disposal.

Tenders frequently must be submitted on official forms, so the structure of the tender is closely controlled. The official form is obtained from the inviting body, along with the terms and conditions, specifications, quantities sheets and any other necessary instructions. You might send a covering letter, but with highly formalised tenders, especially for overseas state authorities, the tender documentation is sufficient. Tendering for large contracts is a complex, costly and speculative business, and major companies in, for example, highway construction maintain specialist departments for the purpose.

A letter to a liquidator making an offer for assets

Dear Sir   [Date]

Liquidation of assets of Orange Paper Co

We submit as follows our offer to buy certain of the
assets of this business.

	£
Paper stocks, coloured cartridge, 6 tons at £250/ton	1,500.00
Two delivery vans at £1,000 each	2,000.00
Miscellaneous office effects as per attached list	250.00
Total	£3,750.00

We will make arrangements to collect these items and
will deliver our cheque into your hands as soon as we
receive your acceptance of our offer.

Yours faithfully

Termination see *Dismissal*

Testimonials see *References*

Thank you letters

It is always pleasant, amid the morning's post and the welter of problems and complexities it brings, to open a letter like the following:

Dear Jim
Just a note to say thank you for organising your
company's presentation to us yesterday. Your
hospitality was of the best. We found the business
discussion interesting and full of possibilities and will
be in touch soon to discuss the follow-up.

So remember to drop little notes to people. It is courtesy to say thank
you after you have been to a special lunch, or been entertained in
someone's home.

Thank you for a birthday gift from your colleagues or staff

> Dear friends
>
> Thank you for your kindness in remembering my birthday! Not that I wanted anyone to remind me of another birthday; in fact I'd forgotten all about it. But what do I care – I like getting another year older among such sympathetic colleagues.
>
> Seriously, I was very touched, thank you all again.

Discreet thanks to supplier who gives you a Christmas present

> Dear Bill
>
> Many thanks for your Christmas good cheer – a very kind gesture. Here's to a prosperous New Year for your business, and a Happy Christmas to you and your family.

A letter thanking a member of staff for good work

> Dear Anthony
>
> I had the pleasure of reading your report last night. I was impressed by the work behind it and look forward to discussing your recommendations when we meet next week.
>
> [or: I had the pleasure yesterday of venturing into the Order Department after your reorganisation. I see from the figures that the work flow has improved and from the evidence of my own eyes that staff morale has gone right up. It just shows that close management

involvement can generate a productive response in
both business and human terms.]

My congratulations on this successful outcome to
some hard work. Your efforts are much appreciated.

Yours,

(Signed)

Trade references

When you have a new customer and you wish to establish his credit
status, the trade references he gives you are likely to be more helpful
than his bank reference. You can take up trade references by phone
– as ever, you will get a more revealing opinion if it doesn't have to
be written down. In most cases you would address your enquiry –
verbal or written – to the credit controller or the accountant. If you
wanted to discuss other aspects of trade than purely debt collection,
you might go through to the marketing manager.

Taking up a trade reference

Dear Sir   [Date]

Norman Clark Grub Screws Ltd

We have recently received our first orders from the
above company, who have given us your name as a
trade reference.

I should be most grateful if you would let me know
whether your trading experience with them is
satisfactory or otherwise; whether you believe them to
be financially sound; and whether you have had any
problems with payment.

I can assure you that any information you care to
disclose will be treated with the strictest confidence
and will not be kept on file.

Thank you for your help.

Providing a trade reference – favourable

Dear Sir   [Date]

Thank you for your enquiry about Jeremiah Chicken
Portions Ltd. I am happy to provide a trade reference
for this company.

They have been customers of ours for over five years
and have maintained a modest but steady level of
business with us. By and large we do not have more
than £1,000 outstanding with them at any time, so I
could not vouch for credit limits beyond this mark. We
have found them to be regular payers, perhaps with a
habit of taking an extra 30 days, but that has not
proved a problem.

Our md is an old friend of their chairman, Mr Jeremiah
Chicken, and there is a friendly working relationship
between the two companies.

An extremely reserved trade reference

The key phrase is to advise caution.

Private and Confidential   [Date]

Dear Sir

With regard to your request for a trade reference for
Floppit Software Corp, I would suggest you exercise
caution.

They have never let us down but on occasion we have
had to wait for our money. At present I am limiting
their total credit outstanding to £500.

Given the volatility of the business they are in, I would
suggest you keep your exposure to a minimum.

A negative trade reference

> Private and Confidential   [Date]
>
> Dear Sir
>
> I am unfortunately unable to provide a trade reference for Waxy Pancakes Ltd. We are currently taking steps to recover monies owed to us.

Or the following:

> Dear Mr —   [Date]
>
> I regret I cannot provide a trade reference for Smith, Jones and Robinson Ltd. Perhaps you would care to telephone me at your convenience.

Warning letters

A warning letter is sent to an employee whose work is unsatisfactory; generally speaking an employee must have received a warning before he can be dismissed.

As ever, it is good management to summon the employee and tell him face-to-face that his work is unsatisfactory – with the reasons why – rather than send him a letter out of the blue. Occasionally people have no idea what standards are expected of them and, if spoken to positively, can improve their performance. Mostly, however, bad workers or shiftless individuals don't change their spots. So at the meeting they are told they are herewith receiving a warning, and a letter will follow in confirmation.

A letter of warning of possible dismissal for poor work

> Dear Harry   [Date]
>
> I am afraid I must write this letter as a warning that your work has fallen seriously below the company's required standards.

Your work entails responsibility for packing foodstuffs.

1. On 13 May you were found smoking in the prohibited area.

2. The checker on the despatch line found 26 instances this week and 11 last week of boxes with your code on which were not properly sealed.

We are all human, and make mistakes. One or two missed boxes is perhaps to be expected and the checker is there to spot them. But your work shows carelessness plus a disregard for hygiene.

Please do your best to work to our company standards of packing and health, otherwise we will be unable to continue to employ you. I will review the situation in one month's time.

A letter of warning of possible dismissal for dishonesty

Dear —   [Date]

You were caught taking money from the petty cash this morning.

I know the sum was small, but honesty and trust are the first essentials in a business.

You have pleaded with me for a second chance, and you shall have it. This letter therefore is a warning that any recurrence will mean immediate dismissal. But I hope that if we say no more about this slip of yours, you will give us good work and good service.

Word processed letters

See also COMPUTER GENERATED letters.

Use your word processor for what it is good at – remembering what you said before, and serving it up quickly. If you have the time and aptitude, and that kind of job, which enable you to compose complex narratives on your screen, fine. Otherwise make sure you have your system set up so you can get letters organised quickly. Standard and semi-standard letters should be saved in an orderly way.

Check on the print quality of your word-processed letters. Off older or smaller or tired dot-matrix printers they sometimes come out so faint you can scarcely take a photocopy of them.

Zippy letters

Keep your letters sparkling. Impart some energy to that dull old correspondence. Be brief. Be bright. Be zippy.

A zippy letter apparently combining business with pleasure

Dear Zoe   1 April

Sales campaign for NEW ZEST sparkling drink

Many thanks for your presentation of the spring campaign for NEW ZEST. The costs are right and we like the zany tone of the campaign.

There is one area which was not adequately covered. In our briefing meeting we wanted to go for the jaded executive/six o'clock drinks market by aiming at housewives with the message, 'Bring NEW ZEST to your man!' Can you revise the housewives space coverage to include a set of ads on this theme?

Revised proposals by Friday, please. The studio is standing by as from Monday and we must keep the deadline. Let's put some zip into it!

Could we discuss the details over dinner on Friday? I suggest you call by here at six and we give NEW ZEST a market test...

Best wishes.

Ziggy